For Andy and Foster with my deepest love

General Disclaimer

The information contained on this book and its affiliated website is educational in nature and is provided only as general information. The complementary healing modalities discussed in this book appear to have promising mental, emotional, spiritual, and physical health benefits but many of them have yet to be fully researched by the Western academic, medical, and psychological communities. Due to the experimental nature of these approaches, and because they are relatively new healing approaches, and the extent of their effectiveness, as well as their risks and benefits have not been proven, the reader is required to assume and accept full responsibility for any and all risks associated with reading this book, practicing the meditations and using any of these modalities as a result of reading this book or any literature on these modalities available through the affiliated website. The reader is required to understand that if s/he chooses to use these modalities, it is possible that s/he may experience changes in physical conditions and/or in emotional or physical sensations or additional unresolved memories may surface which could be perceived as negative side effects. Further physical symptoms or emotional material may continue to surface after using these modalities, indicating other issues may need to be addressed. Previously vivid or traumatic memories may fade which could adversely impact my ability to provide detailed legal testimony regarding a traumatic incident.

The information presented in this book is not intended to represent that these modalities are used to diagnose, treat, cure, or prevent any disease or psychological disorder. Complementary/alternative healing modalities are not substitutes for medical or psychological treatment. Any stories or testimonials presented in this book do not constitute a warranty, guarantee, or prediction regarding the outcome of an individual using complementary/alternative healing work for any particular issue. Further, the reader is required to understand that Anne Bertolet Rice makes no warranty, guarantee, or prediction regarding any outcome for the reader using these healing approaches for any particular issue. Upon starting this book, the reader is required to agree and understand that the information presented in this book is only for his/her own personal use. In order to use complementary/alternative therapies with others, the reader/meditator must understand s/he needs to become sufficiently trained and qualified as a complementary healing modality practitioner. While all materials and references to other resources are posted in good faith, the accuracy, validity, effectiveness, completeness, or usefulness of any information herein, as with any publication, cannot be guaranteed. Anne Bertolet Rice accepts no responsibility or liability whatsoever for the use or misuse of the information contained in this book. Anne Bertolet Rice advises you seek professional advice as appropriate before implementing any protocol, meditation, or opinion expressed in this book, including using any complementary healing modality, and before making any health decision. If any court of law rules that any part of the Disclaimer is invalid, the Disclaimer stands as if those parts were struck out.

Information in this book is not intended to be used in place of medical diagnosis or treatments prescribed by your medical doctor. Please advise your doctor when you use any of the modalities presented in this book so that s/he can be aware of any possible interactive effects with your medical treatments.

Contents

Introduction

This book is devoted to helping all who are facing a physical disease or condition, as well as anyone seeking in-depth healing in mind, emotion, and soul. Welcome and thank you for joining me on this healing journey. Wherever this book has reached you, facing a physical disease or life condition has set you on a search for answers. You are not alone. There are many of us in the world today with physical or emotional challenges, desperately seeking health and peace of mind, yet continually bumping up against limited forms of treatment. "What can I do to heal myself?" we ask. "I know there has to be more to healing than conventional approaches, but where, what, and how do I go about it?"

In this healing series, I will answer these questions by guiding you step by step along the multileveled path of healing disease and disharmony. While this process is not meant to supersede other forms of medicine, it has the potential to enliven whatever course of treatment you are presently on while finding and healing the cause of the condition. This approach speaks to the whole person. Together, we will explore how the mind, emotions, and soul play an integral role in the disease process as well as clear the way to a heightened and healed state of being. Whatever the outcome of our physical condition, this process can enrich our lives and expand our capacity to enjoy our time on earth deeply, fully, joyously.

This healing series is a devotion of the heart, intended to speak to you on all levels. It is an invitation for your mind to open to the concepts introduced, for your emotional self to respond through spontaneous release and fulfillment, and for your body to absorb every word and receive each resonant chord of healing. These words and practices present a way for you to recognize the truth of your spirit's higher reality while opening a pathway for you to experience its healing power in your body and mind. Discovering your healing potential and receiving it into every cell can bring profound transformation if you sincerely choose it.

How to Use This Healing Series

This series is a process; it is a dance between mind and spirit, intellect and experience. Each chapter explores vital aspects of the healing journey followed by a meditation intended to bring healing into form in an experiential way.

As you take in the teachings, exercises, and meditations, allow the process to unfold in you without outer distractions. Whenever possible, prepare a quiet, private space to breathe in the words and concepts, holding in your heart an intention for the highest outcome. Just as much about illness is unpredictable, so, too, is the process of healing. It would be helpful to set aside some time for the subtle realms of self-healing to develop.

The teachings and meditations were written to complement each other. The readings highlight some of the most vital points of the deep heart healing path, placing the experience of healing in a clearer context of understanding. The teachings present insights for healing, and the meditations call them to action. As you experience necessary shifts in perspective and reality through the teachings, the practical experience will bring forth the deep medicine that grounds healing into the body, mind, and soul.

I have incorporated into the teachings, where appropriate, personal examples of transformation and healing, including my own. While names have been changed for the sake of privacy, the stories are true and serve as examples of what is possible for each of us.

Each chapter builds on the previous one and prepares the seeker for further depth and healing. Allow as much time as you need to integrate each step before moving on to the next. Some meditations will hold a deeper resonance for you than others at times. Explore again and again the ones you feel most drawn to as many times as you are called to do so.

The first four chapters are written to guide you through the release of the density and disharmony of your humanity. Chapters five through nine are a celebration of the subtle realms of light and bliss and breaking through into higher realms of consciousness. We each exist on all levels at once. Where you are most identified in any moment should be your guidepost as to which chapters and meditations you choose to focus on at any given time.

Igniting the Heart and Becoming the Flame

The purpose of this book expresses itself in levels, as mentioned above. The first level is the igniting of the heart. Upon first starting the path we come to realize that conceptual learning to satisfy the linear thinking of the reasoning mind is only a small part of the journey. Soon it becomes clear that the path begins to open a communication with the deep knowing within our heart's essence; it awakens a connection to the spirit

within our heart and invites it forward into our awareness, body, and life. At times, especially if this approach
is new to you, it will not make immediate sense to your
critical left-brain functions. Give it time. If approached
sincerely, this process will form a synthesis between the
heart and the mind. As the heart educates the mind, an
intuitive integration of the experience comes, whether
upon first absorbing this material or months later. The
innate intelligence of the heart, I have learned, seam-
lessly integrates these teachings in a deep and personal
way.

The second level is the act of becoming. It is a surrendering of all that holds us back from living in con-
tinuous communication with our inner guidance and
releasing the pain that creates a perceived separation
between us and the Spirit of The Love.

The final level is one of being. There is no separation between us and Spirit. We are One in complete
harmony regardless of outer circumstances or even our
habitual impulses toward separation. Here we have
reached critical mass and are in Unity. Healing takes
new meaning as the purpose of our conditions are
held from a higher truth, a more comfortable reference
point. All is joy.

I offer these teachings to those of you who feel called
by your hearts to follow a path that whispers to you

from realms beyond the linear mind, whether such a path is new to you or is a continuation of a long, familiar journey. This "himma," or longing for God, arises as a deep, intuitive trust that this work *feels* right, and therefore *is* right for you. As you digest this material, I invite you to entrust your "reasoning" mind to your heart, and trust that the answers will come.

When I first stepped on this path, I had no idea where the teachings were leading me. I only knew that they felt completely right and were perfectly aligned with my deeper purpose. I realized that I would never go back to my life as it was. I received morsels of left-brain clarification when they encouraged a deeper surrender to the process. However, once I digested these teachings, the finer elements were unveiled through my heart's personal insight and intuition. I found that, once absorbed by the feeling heart, the mind will catch up, step by step, with its higher intelligence.

I have come to appreciate this method of learning through personal experience. I studied Sufi texts that were seemingly so obtuse that anyone trying to read them using the left brain would be boggled. We students were often given the writing assignment to copy the passages word for word. When we did this, our minds could let go and our hearts could open to the intuitive message and telepathic communication within the text. In those moments, the insights that welled from my heart taught me more than I could have received from lifetimes of scholarly study.

While the teachings in this book are presented in a simpler, more accessible manner, questions will still arise. Hold them close and ask for the answers to come from your heart. As you trust, surely they will appear through your own insights, as well as the experiences, books, and conversations you will draw to you.

I offer these teachings and meditations humbly, hoping to give you the same opportunity for depth that I was given, to those souls longing to receive it.

May you find your deepest blessings in health, and your soul's true calling.

Acknowledgments

I extend my love, gratitude, and appreciation to my teachers, Ann Conover and Kamil and Kamillah Nash, who carried the torch for me at the start of my journey into the deep heart, guiding me through the darkest night into the subtle and sublime.

A special thanks goes to Ann Conover, my spiritual sister, who has been by my side through it all with an incisive wisdom and a depth of commitment to truth and acceptance that continue to inspire me.

To my husband, Andy, for his devotion and commitment to our lifetime of love and marriage and for lighting my fire through his humor, passion for life, and the art of play!

Andy's technical mastery and support not only brought *The Healing Power of the Deep Heart* into book form, his support of my writing inspired this material from the start.

To my son, Foster, for making life a continual adventure of enthusiastic discovery and for lighting my heart ablaze with such indescribable love.

To my parents, for a lifetime of love, laughter, and growth together.

To Michelle Lefevre, for her integrity in business, her inspired role in laying the groundwork for *The School of the Deep Heart* and the conception of this book, and for bringing laughter and a light touch each step of the way.

To Tinker Lindsay, for her open mind and intuitive and incisive style, and for helping to bring this book to completion with richness in mind and heart.

To my mother-in-law, Maggie, for her graciousness, caring, and generosity.

Thank you to all of the health practitioners who have brought their own distinct insight and support to my healing journey. Their modalities include: Chinese medicine, homeopathy, naturopathy, iridology, yoga, network chiropractic, deep tissue massage, craniosacral, and whole system nutritional cleansing, among others.

My deepest gratitude goes to The Presence of The Love.

Author's Note

There are aspects of healing that have not been included in this book because they are broad subjects or because they are simply not a part of the subject matter in this text. One of these is sexuality. Sexual energy is a potent way to move stagnant energies in the body when directed with consciousness. If you feel called to study the healing path of sexual energy, I recommend reading Eastern texts on healing through Tantra. There are many to choose from.

Physical exercise is another topic that is of importance in healing that was not included in these pages.

As always, where your heart leads, follow!

Chapter 1

Finding Our Way Home

What if you were told that there is a place in your being, that once accessed, could heal you of all your ills completely? What if you were told that once you open this door inside yourself, you will unleash miracles and an unveiling of the mysteries in life? Would you open the door? Would you turn away? The choice is yours.

Choosing to Heal

> *Take your chance, beloved!*
>
> Sufi Sheikh Sidi Muhammad

Deep inside, we know there is a sacred meaning in disease, even if we have not been able to put this feeling into words. We have a choice in how we face and treat our human conditions. We can choose to heal by finding the deeper significance in our challenges.

Maybe physical disease, a difficult mental or emotional condition, a troubling relationship, or simply an uneasy feeling has called you to stop and reevaluate your life. Perhaps you've decided that you are no longer going to give in to your illness or life situation. You may question if there is more you can do to get well. Whatever brought you to this point in your life, things as they stand cannot comfortably stay the same. The good news is, this condition you find yourself in holds a message, specifically for you. You might feel like it's written in hieroglyphics, but the contents are yours to decipher. This message is an unmistakable invitation to change, presented in a manner not to be missed. Your mind may be asking, "Couldn't it have arrived in a little easier or less painful form?" But the clearest place within you knows that regardless of the outcome, this experience has deep meaning for you.

While resistance to the notion that suffering has a purpose is common, how many of us have started psychotherapy, meditation, yoga, nutritional cleanses, or a spiritual path because we were happy? We are called to action by our problems, catalyzed by discomfort to find meaning in our existence. Our problems invite us to discover the significance behind what is being presented to us. Our life situation is always an echo of the hidden plan within our human design. Embedded in the specific challenge you now face is an invitation to discover the meaning within the mystery of your disease or life condition.

Your healing journey may have begun with a persistent sense that what is happening to you holds significance in your life, and that it is here to teach you something. Perhaps you are merely curious to know more about your situation. Maybe you feel called to heal your condition from the roots up, to discover all that there is to know about this experience of disease and the release from it. Maybe something someone said struck a deep chord, or your inner voice led you to find a new way, and here you are. Whatever has brought you here, if you have the longing for this path of discovery, and the willingness to go for it, you've already taken the hardest step.

Sometimes lack of passion prevents us from moving forward, beyond this sense of calling. If this is the case for you, I urge you to find your passion. Dig deep. Release the resistance to change—whether with a teacher or guide or through meditation—and move forward. You have everything to gain and nothing to lose.

Once you have discovered the longing or inspiration to heal, the next step is to simply choose it. Choose the path of metamorphosis through your condition. Open like a flower to your inner sunlight. Set your mind and intention on awakening to all that this disease or situation has to teach you. Find the juice for it, over and over again in your heart, and state your intention with sincerity. The healing presence within you will respond in one way or another to your sincere volition. Trust this.

The Deep Heart: The Home of Healing

> *Your vision will become clear only when you look into your heart. Who looks outside, dreams. Who looks inside, awakens.*
>
> CARL JUNG

How do we find this healing power once we feel called to look? Our healing ability is located inside our hearts. The heart is where our humanity bridges our divinity. This deepest place in our hearts, the "Deep Heart," is the portal into dimensions of healing, ecstasy, and all high qualities of being.

The Deep Heart is the conductor of a soft, yet powerful electromagnetic current that moves through each of us in its own unique way. It speaks in a language of feeling, images, metaphors, whispered thoughts, and the experience of resounding peace, love, true power, and all high qualities. When we deepen into these feeling states, the truth about life, self, and existence is revealed. The Deep Heart holds its own strong medicine and can heal us from the inside out.

We all possess this power, what Sufis[1] identify as "The Love," within our hearts. It may also be called the Power of Consciousness, Great Spirit, The Universe, God, Allah, Christ, Buddha-mind, among other divine names. Whatever title we choose, when we experience the heightened reality of its presence in our hearts through *feeling* it, we open to the mystical power of healing from within.

Many find it helpful to evoke a personalized aspect of consciousness, such as Christ. This can lend a depth and power to the healing experience. Others resist the notion that their beliefs must be attached to a particular prophet in order to find healing. My personal experience has been that anyone, with or without religious beliefs and concepts, can heal if they find and feel the powerful sensation of The Love in their hearts. This medicine is here for all of us, at the center of our existence.

We all have the potential to heal ourselves. As Christ

---

1   Sufis are mystics who practice feeling and becoming what they have discerned over the centuries to be the ninety-nine qualities of God, or The Beloved, felt in the heart. Qualities such as compassion, truth, freedom, joy, wisdom, etc. are felt as direct manifestations of God. These sacred qualities are the blood and bones of the healer within.

once said, "You shall do the works that I do, and even greater works than these." The source of miracles is right here, under our noses, just waiting for us to find it. Venturing inside will spark the momentum that sets our healing in motion.

Feeling: The Key to Connection

The best and most beautiful things in the world cannot be seen or even touched. They must be felt with the heart.

HELEN KELLER

The key to unlocking our connection to The Love is simple, yet multilayered. There is one basic element to tapping the inner healing ability that is still, to this day, elusive to many. That one element, accessible to us all, is *feeling*. We must *feel* The Love, or God, in our hearts. Without the evocation of this felt sense, we have very little access to the realm of healing. Opening to the feeling of The Love invites forward the presence of a higher frequency or state of being. This presence has within it all that you have been consciously and unconsciously seeking. With attention, it will grow inside of you and fill you with loving sensation. As the Sufi poet Rumi once said, this presence is the "perfume that we live in."

It is a fragrance that can be felt and breathed into every cell with deep pleasure.

This intimate feeling experience is an eternity apart from ideas or concepts about it. We could spend life-times studying theology and filling our heads with no-tions about The Love and never once actually drink it in. People have plenty of opinions about what God is. Wars have been fought over whose idea was right. At the end of the day, have they reached the answer? Of course not. What we call "God" does not fit into any concept or belief. God is not limited to an image in our minds. God is to be experienced as a state of being —a personal and universal connection. The Love.

You might have your own strong opinions about what God or consciousness is and is not. Let go of them now and simply allow the *feeling* of this warm, healing presence to come into your awareness. Open to receive and feel the gift of its presence now. Let your heart fill with love, warming you from the inside out. The quali-ties of feeling that arise bring your personal guidance and healing ability to life. Acknowledge and honor the power of this vast intelligence in your heart and call it forward to show you the way. Speak to it with sincerity and intimacy. Say, "Show me how to know the guidance and the healing power I need. Show me the way. I am ready." This step, if made sincerely and with conviction, is the first step on your way home. The path and its results are as unique as each individual, and the destination is both profoundly personal and deeply healing.

In many ways, facing a physical or emotional condition can be compared to facing an addiction. Breaking an addiction requires sourcing something more powerful than the addiction itself. Many recovering addicts will attest that for them, accessing this higher power was the only way out of a strong whirlpool that was pulling them under. Disease is no different. The way out of something as serious and life threatening as addiction, disease, or downward emotional spirals, such as depression, self-hatred, and despair is through connecting with and surrendering to a greater will than our own, a power that can overcome any human obstacle. This superhuman power within us transcends the human mind and acts from its own high intelligence. It knows every nuance of contraction or illness our bodies hold, and with our personal will calling upon it, it can bring profound healing on every level. It can pull us from a strong vector of emotion. It can purify a deluded mind, and it can heal any physical condition or disease. All we need to do is learn how to get out of our own way and allow our innate healing power free rein. When we do this, our perceptions change, and we can see the way to our personal healing with greater clarity.

The healing experience of the Deep Heart is real and attainable. There are countless stories of people healing their disease (physical, mental, or emotional) by tapping The Love within. These are people who have accessed their inner healing power and reached heights of health, mental acuity, and spiritual awakening through their conditions. There is nothing more real, rich, full, and freeing than having the experience of healing firsthand. And everyone is capable of it. Everyone.

Rebecca

Rebecca was diagnosed with multiple sclerosis. She started out taking the conventional route of treatment with medication. Then she was told that she had a year to live. This prognosis led to a radical shift in identity for her. Her life changed drastically as she faced the pain and anguish of her disease and the emotional roller coaster that ensued. Rebecca had always had a strong trust in the guiding intelligence of—in her terms—the Lord, and she began to call her guidance forward. She asked over and over again to be given direction and to have help in surrendering to the healing process. Soon, something ignited within her. She began to feel surges of strength flooding her. The presence within her Deep Heart was saying,

"Don't give up! Fight this with all your strength!" She felt motivated to take the reins and to deny her illness any power over her or her life circumstances.

Each step of the way, Rebecca listened and felt more and more deeply guided by the compelling movement of her heart. Her heart became the friend that led the way for her through the pain and into healing. Many emotions surfaced, and her Deep Heart guided her to let them move through her fully. Her strength grew as she released her tears, her anger, and her fear. She learned to trust that she was being held by this very loving, internal presence, while releasing into the healing movement of her emotions. As she grew stronger in her faith, the inner guidance from her heart became more and more clear to her, and continued to lead her to health. With the felt qualities of strength and trust bubbling up from deep inside, she faced the inner conditions that fed the disease process, and chose life instead.

Eight years later, she is still vibrantly alive, still walking her path of miracles. She chose to stop taking medication for her illness, and has been told over and over again by medical professionals that there is no explanation for her stable state of health. Rebecca knows that there is.

Medical Treatment and Healing:
Allowing Room for Both

> *Healing is a matter of time, but it is ... also a matter of opportunity.*
>
> HIPPOCRATES

How to approach our own medical treatment is a personal choice to be made with deep consideration on an individual basis. Many times, a medical doctor, acupuncturist, homeopathic doctor, or other health practitioner comes along, offering a skill or medicine guided from his or her own discerning heart. And we might find that it is exactly what we need to improve our condition as we continue developing a relationship with our own Deep Heart and a deepening understanding of the spiritual purpose of our disease. There is a place and time for every form of healing if your heart is drawn to it.

The veil is lifting from limited approaches to treatment, revealing that we have more power over our physical, mental, and emotional health than we had ever imagined. Health practitioners from different fields, as well as quantum physicists and metaphysicians, are coming to the same realization: We have the awesome potential to heal from the inside out. We have the capacity to find the power of healing within us. It is inside each and every one of us! Once we find this ability and make room for it to do its work, it can bring us into exquisite states of healing and a fullness of life on all levels.

There is much, much more to physical health than identifying and controlling symptoms. For centuries, the esoteric knowledge of healing has been practiced by yogis, spiritual masters, holy prophets, and others on a deep path. Now this knowledge is more and more accessible to each of us, as the collective consciousness opens to this potency.

Whether it is in your highest purpose to heal your physical condition or to move on to the next level of experience through death, know the guide within is what will bring you home, to your highest reality in love wherever you exist.

Chapter 1 Meditation
Finding and Feeling the Source

Now we will flow into a meditation on finding the feeling of this source. This exercise of deepening into the heart may be practiced in idle moments throughout the day as a ritual or as a meditation when you wake up and as you fall asleep at night. This will build the healing energy within the heart. As it grows, so will the potential for you to heal on every level. It is the meditations that ground us and bring this material home. Join me now for the foundational meditation on the healing power of the heart.

Start by finding a comfortable, quiet place to rest your body and take some deep breaths.

Release all tension in your mind, letting go of thoughts.

When relaxed, breathe right into the center of your heart.

Feel the warmth deep in your heart.

Call to mind someone or something you love uncondi-tionally, maybe a child or a pet.

Feel the sensation of love in your heart.

Allow it to grow.

Let go of the image of your loved one now and simply feel the sensation of love.

Feel it fully, every nuance and texture, and bask in it.

When you get distracted, bring your awareness back to the feeling and anchor into it.

Deepen into the feeling.

Let this loving sensation fill you.

This is the portal into the high dimensions of the heart.

Chapter 2

Emotional Medicine

It is in the silence of the heart that God speaks.

MOTHER TERESA

Finding the medicine of the Deep Heart is a personal journey. For some of us, our first time finding and feeling the healing power within the Deep Heart is instant and life-changing. The connection is immediate. Once known, the experience is undeniable and so profound yet ordinary, that the mind might not know quite how to hold it. It doesn't fit into any schema we have. It just is.

Others experience the healing of the heart most tangibly only after opening channels through which it can be expressed. This opening comes with time as we practice the art of feeling the sensations of The Love. What might be a subtle process at first grows into tangible, often astonishing, manifestations as we expand our awareness of it.

Our connection to the Deep Heart might appear in glimpses, perhaps as an image or a word that pops into our mind, yet clearly originates from the heart instead of the head. The Love might appear within us as a full-bodied joy and laughter, a delight in the humor of life's circumstances. We might feel it as a vibration, originating in our heart and moving out through our hands or eyes, or it might be channeled through our voices in tones that carry a healing vibration.

However The Love appears, when we trust it, it often responds with clear guidance and unexpected synchronicities. Our dreams, our experiences in life, and our internal states become linked in one flowing moment of *now*. Our lives might be impacted in ways that we could never have imagined. We want to pinch ourselves to see if it's really happening.

Each moment that we are reminded of our heart's healing power through an experience is a moment to express gratitude. Gratitude fuels a momentum toward healing. Continually taking note of all the subtleties of our Deep Heart and its manifestations further deepens our relationship to it. As we practice connecting to this inner sensation and becoming better acquainted with it, we are able to recognize and welcome it. The more we embrace this healing medicine, the more its presence grows in our life, body, mind, and world.

Dissolving Inner Walls

Managing emotion ... enables us to drink from elixirs locked within our cells, just waiting for us to discover them.

DOC CHILDRE

When we point our internal compass toward the Deep Heart, we are given moments of awakening and clear purpose. Then, just as noticeable are the moments when we feel blocked and unclear. We might feel unable to reach our Deep Heart. The healing process often involves some weed whacking and a lot of excavating. Sometimes our Deep Heart is so buried that it requires a virtual construction crew! But the Love *is* right here inside, waiting to be discovered. The more we grow to trust this and take the necessary steps to get there, the more quickly it will come forward.

Each of us is an intricate web of dimension. Our bodies, minds, emotions, and souls are never separate from each other. Each strand profoundly influences the whole. The many strands are interwoven in a complex, yet elegant design, so that if one aspect is in disharmony, it influences our entire being. When reaching for the healing power of our hearts, setting out with a sincere intention to know our true nature, we often encounter these disharmonies. Sometimes they feel like inner walls that block us and stand in the way. The purpose of these walls is to guard the Great Hall of Love hidden in our hearts. We can find the entrance into the deeper chambers where our healing power resides once we discover what is holding these walls in place.

The treasure we all seek is hidden deep inside, waiting to be discovered. As we walk, step by step, on our inward journey, the walls we encounter will dissolve if we face them with direct and open curiosity. They are only held in place by our unconscious resistance to them.

At this stage of healing, we often come to discover that the most potent remedy available to us is hidden within what we most often avoid: our emotions. Many of us don't consider exploring our emotions to be an option, because we are unconsciously afraid of them. We often deny that they exist, push them away, or, if they come too close, distract ourselves from them. Sometimes we are aware of them, but we are so overwhelmed by their presence that they control us. Yet this avoidance of our emotions is keeping us from the discovery of our lifetime.

Emotions can be seen as a force field surrounding the

very thing we most long for: a vibrantly alive, healthy, love-filled existence. The path to our Deep Heart's treasure, the healing power within, is not around or above, but through this emotional field. Emotions must be respected and felt in order to access deeper levels of healing. Have you ever noticed that those who cry easily also love easily? Those who have a healthy relationship with their anger also feel the most passion. Those who walk through anxiety, instead of avoiding it, find great courage. These higher states are all qualities of our Deep Heart's healing power or The Love.

Most of us were taught early in life to see vulnerability as failure or weakness. This is a common misperception in our culture—that emotions reflect a lack of strength. "Be tough," we are told. "Get a grip. Keep it together!" We all have our own versions of these admonitions. Such statements urge us to contract from, cut off, or ignore our emotions. When you adhere to these demands, you are lopping off an essential part of yourself, experiencing life as a partial person. Your potential becomes stuck in first gear. Unconsciously we might still be choosing to listen to those old tapes playing these "tough" adages rather than giving ourselves permission to have the rich, full experience of accepting whoever we are in the moment. Far from reflecting weakness, embracing our emotions shows true courage.

There might be some emotions that we have little trouble accepting. Traditionally, men feel comfortable with their anger, and women are comfortable expressing sadness. However, there is always that one emotion, in any given moment, that each of us resists feeling at all costs. What is yours right now? Anxiety or fear? Frustration or anger? Vulnerable sadness? Grief? Embarrassment or shame? Guilt? Whatever it is, this emotion, locked away for so long, carries a tremendous gift. Holding it with acceptance and then releasing it can dissolve many inner walls, allowing the healing power of the heart to become more tangible. We can then begin to feel its peaceful presence more fully during our day.

Acknowledging Childhood Emotions

> *Except ye… become as little children, ye shall not enter into the kingdom of heaven.*
>
> MATTHEW 18:3

Our first experiences with emotions occurred in childhood. They often felt too big and scary to us, so we shut them out. However, as adults, we find ourselves still shutting them out, still using the solutions of a child.

Jan

Jan, a woman in her 30s, came to see me for healing work years ago. She complained of feelings of loneliness, lethargy, and a chronic digestive disorder. She had isolated herself in life and had great difficulty making friends and expressing herself openly. When we began to look into the emotions beneath her experience of life, we found shame. As a child, she had been continuously corrected by her parents and judged for her behavior. When she made mistakes, they would often say, "Shame on you." Eventually she took on the shame and internalized it. She stopped expressing herself altogether and abandoned trying anything new.

Jan unconsciously lived out the solutions of the child to avoid feeling ashamed as an adult. She continued to close down, feeling very self-conscious when she talked to strangers. She preferred being alone to the feelings of shame and humiliation that gripped her when she interacted. She even experienced this internal constriction physically. It showed up in her depressed demeanor, stagnant digestion, chronic back pain, and low energy. As soon as we found the shame hidden inside of her, I saw a new light shine in her eyes. This buried emotion had finally been seen and acknowledged.

Over time, Jan opened to the emotion even more, feeling it fully without resisting it. The more we sat in unconditional acceptance for the inner child, who felt so ashamed, the easier it became for Jan to unwind and release her inner tension. She came forward and expressed herself more and more freely. By the end of our time together, Jan's life had changed. She was no longer lonely, connecting with others had become effortless, and her health had improved completely. She was pain free, her digestion issues cleared up, and she was left with more energy than she had had in years. Not only did her outer life transform; her inner connectedness with the peace and love in her Deep Heart grew. She felt deeply guided by her heart and found a sense of self that was secure in this connection.

I have seen many such healings occur when people simply hold buried emotions in the unconditional acceptance of the heart. If Jan hadn't discovered the powerful grip of her unconscious shame, she would still be controlled by it. When we really look at our emotions from adult eyes, when we are really present with them, we can see that they are not nearly as formidable as we remember. As we face them, we might re-experience the fear or the traumatic events we have locked away, and the sensation might be momentarily intense. We might even relive our tragic moments as they begin to heal. But this time, we are able to hold the larger context of the adult we now are, bringing safety, love, and comfort to the child inside who still feels overwhelmed. We can have the broadening experience of finding the solutions of the adult, choosing to come back to a reality that fits who we are now and what we are becoming.

The child, or our emotional self, actually fuels the transforming fire of our healing power. By allowing ourselves to become aware of, feel, and accept our emotions, the feelings of the Deep Heart are much more tangible. In other words, each time we allow ourselves to experience our emotions within a container of acceptance, we have opened a portal to the healing power of the heart. When we hold ourselves with this gentle allowance for all that arises, a merciful balm surrounds us, bringing soothing relief to our wounds.

Chapter 2 Meditation
Held by Acceptance

Let's drop into an experience with the emotional self by exploring some of what might be coming up for you at this time in your in life. We will do this while holding it all in a strong container of acceptance. Allow yourself to witness whatever response you have (or don't have), and let it all be OK. Whether you feel it or not, imagine the strong, yet gentle, arms of The Loving Healer of your heart wrapping around you and holding you in safety. Intend for healing to take place.

To begin:

Take some deep breaths and allow your body to completely relax into the container of your loving heart.

Let go and know that whatever arises is okay.

Bring your awareness to your body now and feel whatever emotion or charged thought is present.

Sit with the emotional sensation with a compassionate presence, completely accepting it as it is. (Refrain from pushing it away or forcing the emotion to intensify through effort.)

Drop in deeper to the emotion and feel it fully.

(Resistance to the emotion might appear in a busy mind or distraction. If this is the case, be unconditionally present with the energy of your thoughts. Feel and name the emotion within the thoughts or the sensations in your body. Is it anger, sadness, shame, fear?)

Sit and feel every nuance, allowing its expression through tears, statements, the tone of your voice, or movements of your body.

Notice any thoughts rejecting the emotion, hear them out and then let them go.

Come back to feeling whatever emotion is still present with complete acceptance.

When you have released the emotion or feel complete, breathe in and relax into your heart. Sit and absorb The Love that is present in your heart and bask in its warmth.

Allow The Love to completely fill your body and mind.

Chapter 3

The Healing Cycle: Release and Receive

Hitting Bottom

Let everything happen to you, beauty and terror,
no feeling is final.

RAINER MARIA RILKE

Since first facing your condition, situation, or disease, you have surely walked through many internal storms and tossed and turned through some long nights. You might have found yourself paralyzed, in a state of shock. Although stretches of time might have passed without thinking about your condition, there is always that undercurrent pulling you back to face it. Maybe you have distanced yourself from others as you've come up against your own mortality, your anger, or your fear. Maybe you feel as if you now harbor an invisible enemy, part of an internal army, with you on the battlefield fighting for your life.

Whether you are facing a disease or some other collapse of life as you know it, I don't have to convince you of how intensely helpless this experience can feel. Often, the emotions surrounding disease are just as overwhelming, if not more so, as the actual physical experience. The same is true of other traumas. Fear might be so palpable at times, that your every cell seems to contract. Anger might surge forward, or simmer and brew, waiting for the right time to explode. This feeling of rawness might eventually become "normal," a deeply familiar sensation. All of it can be so overwhelming. So when the initial wave of denial, anger, and fear drops into an even deeper emotion, it can feel like hitting bottom.

Strangely, this bottom can be more comfortable than the initial struggle of absorbing our new reality. Once we actually land here, and the grief comes, our tears can bring release. It's the kind of letting down that brings relief. A sense of surprise might surface as we realize just how much we had been carrying under the surface. Surrendering to the waves of full-bodied sadness and loss is a deep purging that can leave our cells tingling and our minds open. Then, as the well runs dry for the time being, new strength and purity of heart may surge forward. Sometimes the clarity will resonate with peace or relief. Sometimes love and closeness will come forward for those around us. Sometimes humor might come back into the spotlight, which might surprise us. However newfound strength comes from our heart, these moments can bring deep renewal. They can lift us and those around us into higher spirits, which at this time provides a much-needed respite.

Jamie

One summer, Jamie, a very close friend of mine, had a bad case of bacterial pneumonia. She was in a coma for a month. Her organs began to shut down, and everyone around her was sure that she was leaving us. The doctors said that they had never seen someone come back after reaching this point.

One day I was doing energy work with Jamie and helping her through her despair. I clearly felt through my heart that she had reached a crossroads. She needed to make a choice. She could leave her body, her life, and it's struggles behind her or she could choose to harness her strength in love, come back to this world and face her challenges. There was a poignant moment as she searched for the strength of her heart. I sat in deep prayer and offered the strength of my heart as a reflection to her. When the power of her heart filled her, my body shuddered and I heard her giggle. She had remembered her courage and decided to come back. Little by little over the next few days she made her way back to consciousness. The moment she opened her eyes and saw her family, she beamed at them. It was outwardly visible that her strength and love of life was her guiding light.

In the year that followed, Jamie went through many emotions as she absorbed the reality of her recovery experience. She allowed herself to have her sadness and inner struggle and then returned to her buoyant self over and over again, inspiring all who loved her. She laughed and joked through the healing process, connecting with her heart's strength through her humor. Step by step, joke by joke, she shocked her doctors, who called her recovery unprecedented.

However release and clarity come forward for you, the cycle of grief and relief truly is medicine. There will be somber moments followed by joy. Each revolution brings you deeper and deeper into health. Purging and then choosing to fill up on the life affirming energy that follows draws us toward a heightened reality and an embodied knowing of the heart's tender love of life. There is nothing healthier than this. So let yourself cry, let yourself laugh, and be full in life. You will find that the laughter that comes after release is one of those healing agents that can lift you up and shake off the heaviness of disease. The tears wash us clean. The deep belly laughter lightens the load.

As life moves on, and the next challenge comes, a new mind state will appear. This simply means there is another level to drop into, another "bottom" to hit. As the weight of your mind's worries anchors in, you might feel cloudy for a time until the sand settles again. You might feel yourself shutting down or not feeling open to others. You might feel disconnected, even from yourself, unable to feel much. There is emotion inside, but it might feel far away. This is another, new inner wall. Know that this is all part of a deeper course. You are still you, sitting in the center of this cloud of thoughts.

At the other end of this spectrum, you might feel inundated by emotions, so waterlogged that you are weighed down, sloshing and splashing with every step. Whether you feel disconnected or are drowning in emotion, take some deep breaths and come back to you. Find your Deep Heart and feel its strength and compassion. Ask for its guidance, and open to receive it. Let it lighten your load. You do not have to carry this all by yourself. You have a strong mystical presence supporting you at all times. Whenever you remember to, hand it over. Lay down your burden, breathe, and allow yourself to let go.

Let yourself feel the lightness that comes with this form of surrender, and trust that no matter what the outcome, you and your loved ones are held and loved. Take a few moments now to just be with this supportive quality of the Deep Heart.

This path first activates these emotional levels, and then, often very quickly, can drop into an existential questioning: "Why is this happening to me?" "What kind of God would do this?" "Did I manifest or create this disease?" "Have I failed in some way, and am I being punished?" The answer to any one of these questions, if it instills a feeling of guilt or a mentality of blame, is not complete. No one is to blame. You are not wrong in any way for having a disease. God is not punishing you. The condition you face, whether physical, mental, or emotional, is a wave of change. It is here to transform you and help you find your deeper presence of soul, regardless of the outcome.

Acceptance as Medicine

What you resist, persists.

CARL JUNG

Acceptance for what is, is healing. Resisting emotions—the tears, the anger, the sense of loss—creates more inner pressure and prolonged pain than actually just feeling them.

Acceptance is holding an open, allowing, and compassionate presence with emotion, while giving it room to surface. This process is like a magic potion. If done with sincerity, deeply rooted in the heart, it actually releases the tension and brings clarity instantaneously. Emotions can wash over you like waves; cresting, breaking, and rolling to shore, only to retreat into quiet and stillness until the next wave. You might feel like Hawaii's north shore at times, and that's okay. Even the roughest sea comes back to calm.

Acceptance is powerful medicine. When we awaken to acceptance toward our inner states, the pain dissipates. We can come into peace and drink from the well of our hearts. When we find an open, relaxed state, we can magnetize the experiences, medicines, remedies, and people who support us in different ways.

Sometimes acceptance can be confused with resignation. True acceptance is not complacent or stoic. Giving up, or shutting down and waiting to die, brings a feeling of emptiness. We are "walled off" to the experience. We must allow for the fullness of our inner states in order to find true acceptance. By the same token, collapsing in despair is not true acceptance, either. This state is heavy with compulsive feeling; we can't stop crying or raging. "Looping" is another term for it. Whether we stuff our feelings or dramatize them, either approach is a denial of our emotions. Each of these responses lacks acceptance for them in their original state.

There are simple ways to address imbalanced responses. If you tend to wall off emotion, open to your vulnerability. Allow it to flow through. Give yourself the space to have your emotions. If you collapse into hopelessness or rage and find yourself looping in it, choose, with resolution and courage, to bring your attention to your straight, supportive spine. With an open heart, draw yourself to your stable center. Feel the life-giving support there. You are more than this experience of emotional pain. You are stronger than this momentary glimpse of hopelessness. Buddhists refer to states of emotions as clouds in the sky. With compassionate attention we watch (and feel) the clouds pass through. There is no need to attach to them or to push them away.

Acceptance is one form of the healing power within your heart. While it can be a powerful elixir for transmuting physical illness in some moments, in others it can bring emotional support. The Deep Heart is always ready to offer the medicine you need in the moment that you need it. The question is: are you willing to receive it? Are you willing to accept yourself as you are right now? If the answer is yes, you have taken a leap on the path to healing. Willingness and acceptance are two of the most important steps at the beginning of transformational work.

There might be moments where you find yourself in an angry struggle and hear yourself saying, "I don't care; I don't want this disease. I'm done with it!" The emotional charge behind these thoughts might be strong; so strong that you are convinced by it. In that moment, you might identify rage as your reality: "I hate this. I give up." Let yourself have the experience of this emotional moment while simultaneously feeling the strong presence within your deep heart holding you with love and encouragement. Always call your higher power forward, which will hold you steady and keep you present during the release. Never direct rage at another person. Others may at times provoke our anger but they are not responsible for how we feel. No one can make us feel anything that is not already inside of us. When it comes to physical health, self-responsible anger release is more important than most of us realize. With a straight spine, rooted in a core of strength, empty your anger through your voice, out your stomping feet, through your fists on a pillow. All of these actions can release anger from the body, where it can do damage if repressed. Always, during and after a release, come back to a felt sense of strength and clarity. Let go of every little piece of negativity that arises. This is your chance to be truly free of it.

When I was young, my favorite ways of venting were either screaming in my mother's coat closet or rolling up the windows alone in the car and letting it all out. I'm not sure how sane I appeared in those moments, but it felt good! As I later learned, without knowing it, I had been practicing anger release. I remember wondering why I always felt so much better after one of my closet visits.

Since then, I've helped many people to put expression to their anger and release it as a means of finding their center of clarity and flow. It doesn't always have to be a big expression. It can look like sitting in a chair, hitting a low note, and "toning" the anger out your feet, hands, head, or pelvic floor. But releasing it is essential. Anger creates the perfect environment for any disease to flourish. It can actually change the chemical composition of our fluids and tissues. Daniel Hack Tuke, in *The Elibron Classics*, cites cases where saliva has actually turned to venom in certain people while experiencing fits of rage. When they acted out by biting themselves or others, they developed rabies and other life-threatening ailments.[2]

How amazing that our minds and emotions have the power to do this! How much more profound is the capacity of the Deep Heart to heal all of the places in us that have been lost to our own venom.

Anger, fear, sadness, shame, or whatever emotion you are facing in the moment, is leading you somewhere important on this journey to health. There are many points on this emotional ride where you will reach moments of truth. During these heightened moments, when you have just faced your sore spot directly and have consciously released the charge of your emotions, you come to the end of a road. You are now looking over a cliff. This is an exquisitely precious moment of choice. You can choose to stay with what is familiar by sitting down, recycling yourself through the emotion, and identifying your life as a struggle. Or you can choose to leap into a new level of being. At this precious moment of truth, you are emptied out, and the potent medicine of the deep heart is waiting to pour into you. Every time we empty out our pain, there is more room for heightened qualities of heart to fill us in. If you choose to receive it, this medicine will satu-

---

2   *Illustrations of the Influence of the Mind upon the Body in Health and Disease*, Volume II, Elibron Classics, pg. 95.

rate you with its healing power and offer tremendous gifts.

As you open and allow it in, the forms of healing that you can experience in this moment are unlimited. A peaceful presence might enter your awareness; a soft moment of silence while you allow it to envelop and immerse you in comfort. The moment could bring a sense of knowing that all is as it should be. If you feel helpless or stuck, the acceptance of your Deep Heart will often convey, "So, this is how you feel right now. It's OK to let yourself feel the helplessness. Let yourself fully know what it's like to feel stuck. It's OK to feel it." This is one example of the heart's potent yet simple remedies that can bring release and healing.

Acceptance opens the floodgates to other high qualities of the heart. You might feel an inner authority arise to hold you steady. Or you will have the direct experience that you have all the support that you need on every level. At your weakest, you might feel internally held in strength with a new current of life and vibrancy flowing into and filling your body. In your strongest moments, you might feel the awe of this field of light at work in your body, healing mental habits and physical conditions from the inside out. Subtle sensations scour your cells, purifying anything that is not in harmony. This is a deep, visceral, receptive state. It cannot be fully understood by the mind and its concepts, it can only be experienced.

The more we walk on the path of healing dis-ease in all its forms, physical, mental, emotional, and spiritual, the more we are able to develop a deepening of perspective. We can begin to see that each experience has significance. If we allow it, our eyes can open. We can evolve into the knowing that life is more than physical survival and outer pursuits of money, relationships, good looks, career accomplishments, and other external goals. When the big challenges come, buried emotions surface. Remember, it is a blessing when they do. For when they come to light, they free us from old burdens.

Chapter 3 Meditation
Balm for Our Wounds

This meditation is for those times when we are feeling tender and emotions are on the surface. Here we can allow for the healing balm to soothe and bring the healing quality we are most needing. If this is not your state of being at this time, continue finding support through the meditations in chapters one and two.

Begin this meditation sitting upright on a cushion or with your back supported in a firm chair. Be sure your spine is straight, yet comfortable.

Breathing into the Deep Heart, open to your inner essence of strength.

Feel the power of this solid, supportive, mystical presence in your heart. (If you have trouble feeling it, call to mind a time when you felt your strongest. This will help to access your body's memory.)

Breathe this into your central column now, letting the strength pour from your heart into your spine.

Connect to the earth and sky through this central channel.

Embrace the emotional self or "the child" from this solid presence. Bring an unconditional acceptance to him or her.

Ask the child what she/he needs, and listen for the feeling response. Is it love, attention, respect, etc.?

Call the quality she/he needs forward from your heart and let the child drink in its nurturance.

Expand into this feeling, knowing you are held and loved.

Chapter 4

The Emotional Development of Disease

Camouflaging

Our feelings are our most genuine paths to knowledge.

AUDRE LORDE

A friend of mine, really exploring her emotional self for the first time, exclaimed, "It's just so messy!" It's true. Our emotions aren't always cut and dried. The emotional self is more like a very colorful canvas of swirling finger paints. It also provides a very rich inner landscape once we know our feeling sense intimately.

As children, our emotions could be overwhelming, so we learned to protect ourselves from them. We became more complex, hiding and disguising our true responses, even from ourselves. Many of my clients have said, "I know the emotion is in there, but it's so hard to get to. How can I find it, so that I can just surrender to my heart and find its healing power?" Since we have been keeping certain emotions a secret for so long, it might be difficult to pierce through the camouflage, to see them for what they are when they arise.

Let's explore some of the many ways we camouflage our emotions. Anger, for instance, can be disguised as aloofness, judgment, or arrogance. Fear hides behind overly controlled posturing or anxious habits. Shame wears a mask that is overstated, or disappears under a cloak of invisibility. Unveiling the emotion that lies underneath our behavior or facade is life changing. It can bring an unimaginably fuller experience of connection in our relationships and an openness to life. Camouflaged or denied emotions keep us from the fulfillment of our soul's longing. When we release this burden, we are free to feel the lighthearted joy living in our hearts. As a result, there is an influx of energy that brings healing to our mental, physical, and emotional states as well.

While we camouflage and divert the energy of emotion, we escape to our minds. We intellectualize. We justify and rationalize. We overthink, overplan, and overanalyze. We take an emotion and spin it into worry, judgment, fantasy, projection, blame, or dissociation. In this way, fear often appears as worry, rumination, and criticism, while anger translates to blame, guilt, judgment, force, and dominance. Shame can turn into regret, guilt, and self-lacerating thinking. As we age, these emotional thought patterns become habitual and harden into our personalities. We crystallize, and before we know it, we become fused into a fixed way of being. We lose our range of motion in the world as we squeeze ourselves into our heads, identifying as something much smaller than we actually are.

For example, deep anger about our past usually surfaces in an unconscious way. We might repress it, over express it, or deny it exists, but it doesn't go away. It shows up in our personalities. An example of a very common persona masking anger is "The Judge." We are in this persona, or sub-personality, whenever we are judgmental. Like stereotypical judges on courtroom television shows, The Judge perceives the world through a lens of right and wrong, good and bad, black and white.

When we center in our hearts and take a deeper look, we see the anger within this persona. We can see its foreboding presence and disregard for vulnerability. How much room is there for each of us to freely be ourselves when we are listening to The Judge in someone else and, especially, in ourselves?

We must remember though, not to judge the judge!

We must not judge ourselves for our judgment. This is simply an aspect of ourselves and it usually does not define who we are the majority of the time. We can recognize this human part of us for the stuck thought pattern it is and bring compassion to ourselves in this uncomfortable state of mind. We are not alone with this way of thinking. We can all relate to The Judge in some way. How is it that you experience The Judge inside of you? How does your body feel when you are judgmental? Usually we do not feel free to be creative and open when we perceive through the judge's eyes. It is The Judge that keeps our authenticity, freedom, and true authority locked away. Anger and frustration fuel The Judge inside of us and hold this mind-set in place. We can all call to mind experiences when we were exasperated by a person or situation and reacted out of judgment. "You're wrong, Im right!" While evaluating ourselves and others inside our heads, our anger stagnates in our bodies and this directly affects our physical health.

When we heal the judge with the conscious heart, an alternative to the judgmental mind-set arises in compassionate discernment. Suddenly there are more synapses connecting with harmonious ideas and understandings. The jagged quality of the evaluative mind becomes smooth and soft with an ability to perceive the human condition underneath the other's behavior and respond from a larger context of being. The stress of this inner conflict dissolves and our bodies feel more relaxed and alive and healthy. Taking a look at our denied anger is a small price to pay for this profound form of rebirth.

The Judge is only one example of the extent to which we deny the purity of our emotions, even to the point where we become something that we, in essence, are not. Other false personae include: The Controller, The Rebel, The Victim, The Perpetrator, The Pusher or Slave Driver, The Slave, The Seductress or Seducer, The Holy One, The Know-it-All, The Joker, The Chameleon, The Boss, and The Fighter. We could add to this list, but you get the idea. These are all sub-personalities, false versions of each of us.

Personality structures feel concrete, but in fact they are built on a moving foundation. The ground underneath is liquid emotion. When we get down to the basics, let ourselves feel the original emotion and come back to our essential self, The Judge and other personality structures can dissolve and wash away. This leaves us with a fresh, new feeling: a new beginning, a freedom of motion and authenticity. It brings us closer to what is real inside of us and to the gifts of healing within our Deep Heart.

Energetic Restoration

> *Not in entire forgetfulness and not in utter naked-*
> *ness but trailing clouds of glory do we come.*
>   WILLIAM WORDSWORTH

Before we developed personality structures, there
was a fluidity, a lightness to our being. As children,
we experienced it as a full, active river of life running
through us. We played freely with an uninhibited flow
of expression. We all start out with a highly sensual,
innocent, authentic, and deep connection to the source
of The Love.

As we grow, we experience the love in our surroundings and our hearts bond in deep recognition with our
families and guardians. Emotional and mental challenges and soul patterning also come forward from
inside and are met on the outside by those in our surroundings. Traumas or painful experiences result and
form energetic dams inside our bodies and minds. As
we age, the current of consciousness begins to flow
around these blockages. At least some of the openness of childhood is eclipsed by conditioned ways of
being. This process of crystallization, often into sub-
personalities like The Judge, further inhibits the flow
within us.

While the absence of movement, flow, and light begins the process of stagnation in some areas of our bodies and minds, other parts remain absorbed in the joy. Within this dichotomy, we can live life feeling generally good and healthy, while at the same time, there are stagnancies within us that promote disharmony—emotional, mental, and physical. This process manifests in each one of us differently. Some might have more inner stagnancy and manifest only slight symptoms in their body and life. Others might be open for the most part, and yet a small internal block creates a physical condition or painful circumstances. Just as each finger print is unique, so is our personal road map to health. Even very integrated spiritual masters have developed disease and other challenges. Dis-ease arrives in our lives not because we are doing something wrong, but because it is the next step necessary for our personal growth, in line with our very individual and unique life's purpose. *There is a spiritual purpose to every manifested condition, and part of the journey is in discovering it.*

The DNA of Disease

> *Every human being is the author of his own health or disease.*
>
> BUDDHA

For now, let's explore this question: From an energetic perspective, what is disease?

Mental and emotional blocks, our inner dams, actually coagulate, and over time affect the body by forming pockets of illness or disease. In other words, emotions and negative beliefs are the glue that create and hold physical disease together. As scientist and scholar Gregg Braden states, "Western science has now shown without a shadow of a doubt that for every emotion that we create in our bodies, and for all the feeling we create in our bodies, there is a chemistry that matches that feeling. Some of that chemistry is life affirming... and some of it is life denying." The healing power of the Deep Heart is the agent that can reverse life denying chemistry and the process of degeneration and bring rejuvenation and regeneration. Getting to know ourselves well leads to cleaning house of all identification with disharmony, which includes disease.

There have been studies performed by the Institute of HeartMath[3] on HIV positive patients, researching the effects of feeling states on DNA. The research revealed that subjects generating feelings of love, gratitude, and

3   The paper was entitled, "Local and Nonlocal Effects of Coherent Heart Frequencies on Conformational Changes of DNA" by Glen Rein at The Institute of HeartMath.

appreciation produced 300,000 times the resistance to the disease than subjects without these feelings. Likewise, similar studies revealed that DNA responded to stress, fear, and anger by becoming shorter and switching off many of its codes. When feelings of love, joy, appreciation, and gratitude returned, the DNA strands lengthened, relaxed, and unwound. The author of these scientific studies, Glen Rein, wrote implicitly, "Those trained to generate feelings of deep love at will were able to change the shape of their DNA."[4]

This might be a new idea for you, and a hard one to absorb; that physical disease is, on the most fundamental level, a result of our emotions and ingrained negative beliefs. We are not accustomed to holding such an approach in our outwardly focused culture. However, in my experience, and those of countless other healing professionals, acting on this truth is the most powerful way to achieve health and maintain it. It is also the strongest preventative medicine I have come across. Those who develop a strong connection to the higher feeling states of the Deep Heart while purifying their emotions and negative mind-sets, move closest

---

4   For more information on the effects of love and emotion on physical and psychological health, visit HeartMath.org. Another good source is the book *Molecules of Emotion* by Dr. Candace Pert.

to the possibility of deep physical healing. A healthy, harmonious mind and the release of emotional states of being leads to a vibrant, alive, disease-free body. It is both truly miraculous and somehow ordinary when someone steps on this path and undergoes such a deep transformation that disease simply dissolves. On this conscious path, I have both witnessed and learned of many who have experienced the healing of conditions such as chronic pain, life-long allergies, arthritis, cancer, AIDS, digestive problems, phobias, sleep disorders, anxiety and depression, attachment disorders, chronic fatigue syndrome, MS, heart disease, and others.

Just as we mask emotions with different personae, we might also manifest repressed emotion through different forms of illness. For instance I have found that heart disease, on one level, is related to stored anger and fear, and underneath that, loss, longing, and a need for safety. Cancer has been associated with an old, buried resentment that covers issues of trust and a deep hurt. MS is related to issues with control and betrayal, and underneath that, anger and helplessness. Each disease manifests differently, depending on the particular challenges faced early in life, our life decisions, and our spiritual purpose. Within any physical disease, different emotions are found on different levels.[5] Let's pay another visit to Rebecca.

Rebecca

Rebecca, faced with her diagnosis of MS, took the bull by the horns. As she stepped onto her healing journey, many of her buried emotions surfaced. She looked for ways to release them and find the truth of her strength underneath the struggle. Her close friends, about to remodel their kitchen, mentioned that they were going to start demolition soon. When the morning came, there was Rebecca, bright and early, ready with a sledgehammer. She was all they needed, their one-woman demolition team. That day, she released rage with great intention and determination. No longer would she let this destructive force take over her body.

The intuitive guidance of her Deep Heart led the way for her, showing her just what was needed. With clear focus of intention, she externalized and began to release the rage that was within the cellular structure

---

5 Louis Hay provides an extensive list of conditions and their corresponding emotions and belief systems in her book *You Can Heal Your Life.*

of the disease. Allowing for this movement brought Rebecca the initial purging that her body needed and set the stage for her to continue cleaning out her deep-seated condition. The courage to face her anger and to find her strength of heart is the grace that filled her when she made room for it. Demolition day was a turning point for her. The quality of her Deep Heart that she now possesses a thousand-fold since, is strength. She made the choice to embody her power and steer the direction of her disease rather than be its passenger, along for the ride.

Rebecca continues to allow for the healing to take place in whichever way her Deep Heart guides her, and she continues to release deeper levels of her disease. It is an ongoing process, and one that has brought many gifts. Her strength and trust have grown. She has opened to her inner guidance so much that her diet has changed to become more supportive, and she has begun exercising and doing yoga. In letting her healing power lead the way, her passion for life has returned.

Like Rebecca, once we release these more deeply stored traumas in our bodies, we can let go of our personal histories, as well as the emotional imprints of our ancestors. Hereditary conditions that appear in our

DNA can cease to manifest when we relax into the high states of love in our hearts. Opening up, releasing and thoroughly resolving the emotions held in our bodies, can bring such life and rejuvenation that we wonder what took us so long to do this in the first place! Most of us don't even know that it is an option.

Keep in mind that when we venture into the places in us that have been isolated and rejected for so long, opening to the flow of life can come slowly. At first, the physical sensations and emotions might be subtle, or we might be unaware that they are sitting in our bodies, waiting to be discovered. After bridging the light and healing power of our hearts to diseased cells, we might become aware of some physical and emotional pain in the area that is holding the concentration of disease, like a frozen toe when first exposed to heat. The numbness turns to pain as blood and warmth return. The pain is a sign of a renewed flow of energy. Feeling the pain, allowing it, and giving it space to fill out with new life is an essential element in the healing process. And all physical symptoms, whether originating from this form of healing or not should always be monitored by a trusted medical or alternative health professional.

Chapter 4 Meditation
Beneath the Mask

Before starting this exercise, take some time to think about which personae you identify with most at this time in your life.

Let's start by taking some deep breaths.

Feel your strong, deep heart.

Feel The Love here in the center of you.

Feel how this is you.

This center point of all high qualities is the truth of who you are at the essential level. Now, from the eye of your heart, look out at the periphery of you, becoming aware of your personality self, the mask you wear that surrounds your core of light.

What do you see?

What does it have to say about itself?

How does it perceive life?

What is the emotion beneath it?

Sit with the emotion now in a compassionate embrace. Allow it to express or move in whatever way feels cathartic and brings a thorough release.

Hold the wounded child that lives in this pain, and give her all she needs from your loving heart.

Receive the high qualities streaming from your inner source into every cell.

Feel this authentic version of you.

Chapter 3

The Spiritual Origin of Disease

The Secret Source

And now here is my secret, a very simple secret: It is only with the heart that one can see rightly; what is essential is invisible to the eye.

ANTOINE DE SAINT-EXUPERY, *THE LITTLE PRINCE*

As we pierce into pockets of emotion with the conscious focus of our hearts, we might be surprised by what is revealed. Sometimes a memory surfaces, sometimes we see a metaphorical image that means something only to us. We might hear phrases or words, or simply have a knowing that is clear and concise. Through the process of dropping into emotion and coming out the other side into truth over and over again on a deeper level each time, we begin to reach into the spiritual realms. The Deep Heart opens our meditative awareness as we continue to focus our intuitive vision deeper and deeper inside. Eventually we develop the inner vision and aptitude that sages talk about. As this happens, we are able to see the source of our egos'[6] origin. This depth of stored emotion can be compared to a cell. Within its nucleus is the core of our suffering, the secret source of lifetimes of pain. Here is where we house the misperceptions of our soul. Once we reach this center, we sit face to face with the building blocks of disease and disharmony, as well as the ability to heal them completely.

On deep, unconscious levels, we have separated from ourselves and forgotten who we are. We've forgotten that we are always evolving, that we are loved beyond measure, and that there is no separation between us. We are all One. Misperceptions about our very nature have developed into the illusion of pain and suffering. When we drop in so deep that these misperceptions are set free, so are our souls. The bondage that keeps us repeating the same old patterns is finally released, and we are suddenly riding a flow through life, realities apart from the life we lived before. Misperception has a very deep purpose. On an existential level, misper-

---

6   Ego, as referred to in this book, is defined as: All aspects of the self, such as the mask, the sub-personalities, the child, the lower self, that have not yet found integration with the deep heart.

ception—manifesting as disease and disharmony—is an expression of the soul's longing for completion and spiritual evolution. We chose to experience this disease or condition before being born into this world.

"Wait a minute," you might say. "My soul chose this? The deeper part of me wanted to experience this?" Yes. We, our souls, chose to experience our circumstances in childhood, our process of maturing and aging, and we have chosen this condition or disease. You might question, "But why in the world would I actually want to experience this? I wouldn't dream of asking for it."

These responses come from the human personality that sees life as a random experience, without a deeper purpose. They result from our identification as victims, both to the disease and to life experiences. Such misperceptions, until faced, hold power over us. At this point, many people stop the healing process. We can choose to stay with a mentality of limitation and victimhood. Or we can choose radical self-responsibility and radical self-honesty. With the realization that we have a choice comes a poignant moment of understanding that there are no limitations other than those we place on ourselves. This is liberation! We can manifest a different life, one that is a harmonious flow of life force and grace. We can walk a different path if we are open to seeing the bigger picture. This might or might not mean that the disease will be cured. The difference is in our relationship to the disease, to ourselves, to life, and to existence.

We exist on a spectrum with a depth and breadth light-years beyond the limited perception of our own egos. Our beliefs plant us in one little spot, build a cement igloo around us, and leave only a tiny peephole through which we perceive existence! How exciting that we have the ability to step outside this igloo of limitations and open to the wonder and expanse within and around us.

Misperceptions

> *The real voyage of discovery consists not in seeking new landscapes but in having new eyes.*
>
> MARCEL PROUST

Our souls' perceptions are based on how we view God, ourselves, others, and life. These four viewpoints can either open or close us to higher perception. Some dimensions to our souls are aligned with the truth of existence; these produce harmony, unity, and pleasure in our lives. Other dimensions, in which our souls are lost in misperception, draw challenging experiences toward disharmony and disease.

Misperception has a profound impact on every aspect of experience. When I was a child, I pictured God as a gray-bearded male figure that lived "up there" watching over me. As a young adult, I developed other concepts that superseded this image, but my original perception was still stored in my inner files until I uncovered it.

As I grew in awareness and found my way into the Deep Heart, I realized how debilitating this simple, unconscious misperception was in my life. The reality I lived in put God, or The Source, outside of me. This belief drove me to look for all I needed "out there." There was always something that I wanted to have that was out of reach, whether it was good health, a loving relationship, rewarding work, etc. I was frustrated, disappointed, and ashamed. "Why can't I ever have what I need?" I asked myself in exasperation.

The answer came when I experienced a felt realization of how my misperceptions colored my life. With one of my beloved teachers, I had my first direct experience of being connected to all of life through my heart. My perception opened, and insights poured through me. From infinite angles, all at once, I saw how my beliefs were standing in my way of a deeply personal and rich ongoing inner connection. What shifted for me in that moment is beyond words. From then on, I changed my direction and began venturing inside for the sense of fulfillment, love, and ease that I needed. I finally unplugged from the compulsion to chase the carrot! This deeply transformed my relationship with myself, others, and life. It was the turning point, as I slipped into a state of knowing that the ocean of God is in, around, above, beneath, and through me. There is no separation.

Misperception, held in the recesses of our minds, denies us what we yearn for most: a felt sense of the most sublime textures of love. True life is complete absorption in The Love, The Loved, and The Lover that is you in your essence. It is not separate from you; it is you.

The Soul's Longing

> *There is no difficulty that enough love will not conquer; no disease that enough love will not heal; no door that enough love will not open; no gulf that enough love will not bridge; no wall that enough love will not throw down; no sin that enough love will not redeem.*
>
> EMMET FOX

Healing our fragmented perception with the unified field of the Deep Heart is the most essential way we have to live life. What returns with this depth are the parts of us that were lost. Finding and integrating our-selves into the intricate puzzle of life is all that matters. This is what the soul most yearns for. As we complete the picture, we replace separation with love. It expands into our physical form so that we can embody this di-vine, transcendent state. The high presence within us knows how to infuse every little dark pocket inside of us with a permeating, healing vibration. The Deep Heart gives us the opportunity, through mental, emo-tional, and physical conditions, to live in harmony and bring love into every cell.

Mirabelle

While still a student of energetic healing, I worked with Mirabelle, who had chronic arthritis. She was so limited in her movement that it took her a long, excruciating time to get out of bed each morning. Her knees, especially, gave her trouble.

During one session, we discovered a pattern of overwork. Mirabelle found that she subconsciously felt overburdened and unloved. She worked herself "to the bone" every day. This pattern had begun in relation to her parents in childhood. She was raised in a poor family with a commanding father and a subservient mother. The children most valued by her parents were those who worked the hardest. As a child, Mirabelle received the most love and affection after proving herself in this way. Mentally, an inner dialogue emerged between two sub-personalities: The Slave and The Slave Driver. She internally berated herself with harsh commands and outwardly responded to them with meek subservience. Sixty years later, Mirabelle realized that during all this time of pushing herself, she had unconsciously believed that the only way to get love was to work for it! Her joints embodied these feelings of longing, love deprivation, and being overwhelmed.

Becoming aware of her longing for recognition and love was very freeing to her. Her soul's misperceptions became clear as she dropped into her heart to receive the love she craved. She had believed herself to be unlovable and undeserving, God to be demanding and punishing, and the world to hold only scarcity. As I did some hands-on healing work with her, she soon felt the love in her own heart. We invited it to move into her body after some time. Actually feeling the warm current of love move from her heart to her knees brought her an immediate healing. After the session, she jumped up from her chair in amazement; her debilitating arthritis was gone. She not only re-

*leased her arthritis, she discovered the presence of her
healing power and all the love she'd ever longed for or
needed inside of her. Mirabelle recognized the truth
her arthritis was serving her to find, that love is present for her regardless of what she believed.*

As a student healer, this experience made quite an
impression on me. I had heard about such healings, but
it was another thing entirely to witness it firsthand. I
walked away from that session forever changed. It gave
me a deep trust in the power of the conscious heart and
an awe of the miraculous healing source within us. I
have since both personally experienced, and witnessed
in many others, what some refer to as miracles. From
my own perspective, and that of other conscious healers doing this work, healing is simply a natural outcome
of surrendering to the love of the Deep Heart. Healing
unfolds on many levels. If it is what your spirit most
deeply longs for, and if you choose to follow this longing, physical healing will be the end result.

Often, Deep Heart work heals us over time, with
a building of momentum. Other times it can happen
quickly. But this work is not a band-aid that serves to
cover up symptoms. It is a new way of approaching life.
It is a path that creates openings on all levels of our
humanity and leads us to our deeper nature. It goes to

the very root of the illness or disease while dropping us into a new relationship with Love and ourselves. And as we witness the pure precision of this healing agent at work within us, we can begin to see there is more to life than mere survival. The deeper we go on this path, the less identified we become with physical existence. As the fulfillment of the soul becomes our true focus and our deepest medicine, we might even heal our fear of death.

Chapter 3 Meditation
Unveiling Misperceptions

This meditation touches on levels that reach into the feelings of the soul. Feeling deeply into the wound and beyond into the misperception takes sincere intention. Ask your heart if you are ready for this step. If your heart expands in confirmation, ask for help from the source of your light to find your perception's deeper meaning. If your heart contracts and reveals that now is not the time, come back when you are certain that you are ready.

Find your meditative center, deep within your heart.

Ask it to take you to your core misperception. It will be located close to the heart center in your body.

Not thinking about it, feel its disharmony and pain.

From this dark pocket of stored perception, find its identification with a false reality by asking these questions and feel the answers:

What do I believe about God?

What do I believe about life?

What do I believe about myself?

What do I believe about the world/other?

Sufis call these misperceptions "veils." They keep us separate from our light.

Now center in your Deep Heart and call forward the wisdom of love. What is the highest truth about God? Self? The world? Life?

I love myself because I am …

I love God because He/She/It is …

I love life because it is …

I love the world because it is …

Bask in the reality of The Love and receive it into every cell.

Chapter 6

The Healing Truth within Darkness

Peeling the Onion

Perhaps everything terrible is in its deepest being something that needs our love.

RAINER MARIA RILKE

We walk the road to health one awakening at a time. Buddhists compare this process to peeling an onion, removing the skin layer by layer within ourselves, until we reach the sweetest center of existence. With every layer we peel off, we move closer to our personal ecstasy. The closer we get, the clearer our purpose becomes, the cleaner and healthier our bodies and minds are, and the more joyful our experience of unfolding. As we step through each level of emotional/mental configuration, we open into higher consciousness. We begin to embody more intuitive awareness, a state of exquisite clarity and sensation.

Approaching this core of light is, essentially, walking closer and closer to a permeating vibration of white fire. It burns through the film of perception. It eats through negative mind-sets. It vibrates in a depth of sound, rattling and morphing dense emotion and disease states into higher frequencies of feeling. As a result, our physicality breathes life from the essence of this profound presence. Any physical healing we experience originates from these deep inner planes of resonance.

As we peel back the layers of our humanity, or our ego, on this quest, we discover places within us that have remained buried for eons. The closer we come to the great inner light, the more these darker aspects within come forward for healing. Deep inside the shadowy realms of self, we find that in certain places, denied emotion drops into darkness. In this state of separation, we are out of touch with the truth of our vulnerability and in denial of our origin. When we are stuck in this inner pocket, we might sink into mind states that are devoid of rich connection with others and love. The emotional atmosphere within this place feels stark in its empty blackness. Seemingly, there is no end to the bleak state in our minds; we just keep falling. This lower aspect of our personality holds some of our most harmful misperceptions, statements like: There is no God; I hate life; I hate myself. Some of us might experience this state often, while others only in moments. Either way, it is an experience that everyone has tasted.

The Lower Self develops in childhood. When we had no other way of defending ourselves or meeting our needs, we pulled out "the big guns." The Lower Self was our last-ditch effort for some semblance of power when we were at our most vulnerable, false though it might be. This aspect of self represents our defenses dropped down a level, collapsed or hyper-charged in darkness. Yet this part of each of us is only this, a part. It is a fabrication of the ego. The Lower Self is not who we are or even who we were. We might attach to it for a sense of perceived security at certain painful junctures in life, but it is part of our illusion. It does not comprise the Real Self that we are in our Deep Hearts. It serves us to find it.

When visiting this deep inner abyss, it is important to face it from the brightest, strongest light of your heart, the power of your true self at your core. Let your heart infuse your spine with strength as you literally come to center. It is healthiest to give this dark perceiver a moment to express while turning your heart's powerful gaze in its direction. The power of light and love in the center of your heart can then reach out to any place within your body or mind that feels lost in this shadow, firmly bringing it back into the fold. It is crucial that this darkness does not stay hidden from view. Once we expose the shadow, truth can take the reins once again. The deep heart is infinitely more powerful than this mind state. Make the choice over and over again to bask in the warmth of the inner light and pull your reality from the small confines of this stagnant swamp that seeks to dominate your mind.

The Lower Self is the channel through which darker energies enter our minds and our lives. Evil does exist, and it finds its realm of expression through each one of us, through our personal hatred, greed, and malintent. Darkness is born of our wounds. Our weakest states and our most vulnerable misperceptions set the stage for this exaggerated defensive stance. We have all had the experience, at some point, of reacting from hatred while feeling the raw vulnerability underneath it.

As Ann Conover writes in *Adapting to Harmony*:

> *There are two levels of lower self or negative energies that people carry. The more superficial level is the level of negativity. These are energies like blaming, spite, hurtfulness, punishing behaviors, put downs, and destructiveness to self and others.*

The deeper level is the intent to be negative. For most of us, this level is in the unconscious, and we have to dig for it. It's a life-changing experience to find it. Bringing the intent to hurt, destroy, undo, separate, etc., into our conscious mind and emotions removes huge densities from our field, heals unconscious misperceptions about life, frees up our mental and emotional bodies, and makes the way for huge bursts of healing and light to come into our field. As long as darkness is hidden, it remains strong.

Facing the Lower Self

O, happy the soul that saw its own faults.

MEVLANA RUM

It is important to acknowledge the presence of the Lower Self within us. If we remain unaware of our shadow, it has that much more power over us. If we choose to float on the surface of life and present a mask to the world that denies this darkness, our health is at stake. It takes a lot of physical, emotional, and mental energy to keep this kind of force buried within us. Often, what keeps us from facing it is a kind of false pride that claims: "I don't have hatred or resentment, I don't hold onto anything like that." Or: "I know all about that, I don't have to look at that any more." Or: "That's too scary, I'm not going there."

These resistant thoughts keep us from moving forward and getting to know ourselves inside and out, darkness and light. We all contain the entire spectrum inside of us. Claiming to be above it all actually pulls us down into its misery, unconsciously or not. This is not to say that we should let our rage and disdain or our manipulations and harsh impulses for control lead the way. To act and react from this place is harmful. Holding discerning awareness of the Lower Self and acting out with it are realities apart. One way frees us, and the other keeps us in chains.

For those of us facing physical disease, the Lower Self holds a key to the master lock. Behind this barrier is one of the largest inner chambers of life force— our basic life current of health, vitality, strength, and sexual pleasure. This is because our Lower Self leads to the part of us that has an impulse, or a draw, toward death. This aspect of the self can be scary to look at. The movement toward anti-life is something we all hold somewhere deep inside. A physical disease or condition, however, by presenting itself, calls particular attention to this draw toward finality. It offers us the opportunity to heal this dark pull within, to choose to embody life in a strong, vibrant, loving way, in health.

The anti-life element of the Lower Self sounds something like: Life is a burden; I don't care about myself; I don't want to be here; I give up. This belief that destruction holds the power of change we long for is false. The way to transform the darkness is to witness it with conscious awareness, bolstered by the strength and authority of The Love, centered within the Deep Heart. Denying the impact of our darkness on others and letting it take the reins only surrenders our personal power to it.

When we courageously acknowledge this darkness inside, we can choose to love ourselves and others, despite our flaws. It's okay that we're not perfect. As we bring courageous, bold love to the center of our attention, we can hear what it has to say: Life is a gift; Love is my power; I choose to walk home into my core, into my heart, and absorb myself in its certainty and fortitude; I choose life; I am grateful to be here.

Forgiving Our Flaws

Do you want to be a pilgrim on the path to love?
The first step is making yourself humble as ashes.

ANSARI OF HERAT

It takes humility and courage to be so self-honest that we are willing to face both the places within us that we have condemned and the condemnation itself. We might identify ourselves as mild-mannered or gentle and kind. To even consider that there might be a part of us that is aggressive or willfully harmful could be a challenge to our reality. It might turn our stomachs just to think about certain qualities in ourselves and others, yet this is one of the major clues to the Lower Self. This disgust is both the fuel that feeds the fire of disease and the potential key to healing on all levels. We all have unkind places in us. We all have parts of us that we are ashamed of or embarrassed about. Are you willing to recognize that these damaged parts of you exist? Are you willing to forgive yourself for your flaws?

One surefire way to lay bare your Lower Self is to observe what you dislike the most in others. The people closest to us serve as our clearest mirrors, of course. Note your resentment, your bitterness, and your lack of willingness to forgive; be absolutely honest with yourself about this. What traits in others repel you? Just acknowledge this charge you hold. Notice how attached you are to this judgment or disdain as representing the truth. Most of us stop here. We prefer to simply write off the offending person in our minds. But what does that create in life? Does it serve to open our hearts or close us off? Does it invite health or reject it?

Our negativity is not really about the other person. It is a reflection of how we feel about ourselves, about life and about our higher power. Every trait we judge is a mirror of what we reject in ourselves. And at its core is a deep, painful wound. This "flaw" is not the essence of who you are or who the other is. It simply has a hold on you until you pry it loose with loving attention. As you heal your perceptions, your take on what you reject will shift. These traits that once so unnerved you might become endearing, or they might even instigate no charge whatsoever. This does not mean that we need to invite people back into our lives that bring disharmony and pain. We can, however, choose to awaken through the experience regardless of the future of the relationship. Relationship issues are simply an interaction of character traits that serve you to find your way to truth. Are you willing to accept the shameful parts of yourself fully? Are you willing to forgive yourself and others?

Your Defects

An empty mirror and your worst destructive habits,

when they are held up to each other, that's when the real making begins.

That's what art and crafting are.

A tailor needs a torn garment to practice his expertise.

The trunks of trees must be cut and cut again so they can be used for fine carpentry.

Your doctor must have a broken leg to doctor.

Your defects are the ways that glory gets manifested.

RUMI

As we approach the dark corridors in our minds with the translucent fire of our hearts, we are lifted to new heights. Our perception becomes crystal clear, and the negativity we once held as gospel becomes a distant memory or a bad dream we once had. We begin to see how darkness manifests in the world, but we are no longer the predator or the prey in the feeding frenzy of negativity. The eyes of love see the deep meaning behind the darkness. In its highest purpose, this darkness serves to guide us home, to the lighted reality of awe-inspiring love.

Chapter 6 Meditation
The Lower Self

The expressions of the Lower Self range along a spectrum from common judgment to outright war. Are you aware of how the Lower Self expresses in you? Before beginning this meditation, ask the guidance of your heart if this is the right time for you to experience this healing. Trust that you will know when the time is right.

Let's begin by dropping deep into The Love of the heart.

Find your power in light and love and feel it.

Now drop even deeper and anchor into it.

Let it fill you and ground you, like a lightning rod through your spine.

Feel the central column that moves from above your head, all the way down through your base and legs and feet, into the ground.

Hold in mind that the lower self is a wisp of smoke compared to the solid, strong presence of divine power.

Now, allow yourself to become aware of any negativity that you hold in your body or mind. Feel any judgment, resentment, bitterness.

What is the thought that brings the charge?

Look at this negative impulse directly from the strong witness of your heart.

How is it destructive in you and your life?

Briefly let the Lower Self speak and finish these sentences. Do not linger in the negativity, just release it:

I reject myself because ...

I reject God because ...

I reject life because ...

I reject _____ (another) because ...

I want to hurt _____ (another) because ...

(You might feel some remorse, this is a very healthy response if it does not spiral into self-punishment. Send a heartfelt apology on the inner planes to whomever you have harmed, including yourself. Find forgiveness and feel the soothing loving compassion of the Deep Heart surround you.)

Now bring your attention back to your central channel; allow the strength and love in your heart to come forward and fill your spine. This is your real self. This is who you are.

Bring The Love to the vulnerability within the darkness that needs it more than anything.

What is the truth? Finish these sentences:

God loves me because I am ...

I love God because He/She/It is ...

I love life because it is ...

I love the world because it is ...

Drink from this essence in your heart.

Flush out any remaining negativity with this essential elixir.

This is the truth of who you are, all the good in you. This is what is eternal and true.

Begin now to focus on the out breath. Release any tension or toxicity with each exhale. Create more room for your heart to fill you with each inhale.

Feel the love filling you, plumping up every cell in your body with juicy, pink life.

Chapter 7

The Fear of Death

The Purpose of Fear

All fear leads back to the ego's fear of its own death.

ANN CONOVER

What would be the purpose of our fear, if not to open us to our freedom?

By now, you might have become aware of the fear of your own death. This fear has multiple levels to it, of course. There is the physical body's basic instinct for survival, which is grounded in fear. Most of us identify with this fundamental form of consciousness. It perceives mortality as the ultimate end, because to the body, it is.

At the emotional level, death is felt as the greatest of losses. Sorrow and grief rule this domain of fear. We feel convinced that we are forever losing all that has been meaningful to us: our life, our family, our friends, our passions. We fear what will happen next and where we will go after death. It tests our basic sense of security and calls to be held in safety.

On the spiritual level, the soul fears annihilation. It fears losing its uniqueness, simply merging into the infinite, or the finite, and slipping into oblivion as though it never existed.

So much fear. As we unconsciously stall in the fear of death, we forget to live. We let precious moments of life slip by; neglecting to understand that our fear is an invitation to embrace life more fully.

Throughout our lives we are given opportunities to engage in a death and rebirth cycle. When we do this consciously we flow with the soul's natural evolution. This affirmative choice leads to depth of feeling and the exhilaration of embodying spirit anew through each revolution of the cycle. As we surrender our egos and all forms of attachment to life as we know it to the great inner light, we are saying goodbye to self-limiting ways and welcoming a renewal of life. "Die before you die," Sheik Sidi Muhammad has said. Surrendering to the little deaths of the ego while emerging into the true self is how we flow with the micro cycles of death and rebirth. The macro-cycle when the body dies will then be a familiar and joyful experience, the final surrender into the spirit that we are.

Life's challenges draw the choice to renew ourselves or hold on tight in fear of the unknown. Each time we cling on to old ways our ego is facing the fear of its own death. The ego has tunnel vision and is unable to see the broader truths. It is unable to see that when it lets go, its small self is lovingly enveloped in the high self and drawn into a more expansive reality. The death of ego is not a loss. When we let go, the energy that was once invested in staying small, predictable, and restricted joins the dynamic, life-giving river that flows through us. This leads us to become more of ourselves. We feel freer to be who we really are. After the first couple of years of walking on my deep heart path, I remember an old friend of mine insightfully commented, "Anne, you've changed so much and yet you are more yourself!"

The ironic thing about this path of rebirth is that what we most fear losing about ourselves is usually what we gain a thousandfold after letting go. Or sometimes what we fear losing turns out to be less important to us after all. I spoke with a comedian once who said he needed therapy but was afraid it would take his sarcastic sense of humor and livelihood away. What I have noticed is that the kind of humor that alienates others falls away while a fuller, more inclusive, and contagious quality of humor arises. What kind of laughter is more satisfying than revealing the dramas of ego from a unique perspective?

Gratitude

> *Heartfelt positive feelings create far more than a healthy psychological effect. They fortify our internal energy systems and nourish the body right down to the cellular level. For that reason, we like to think of these emotions as "quantum nutrients."*
>
> Doc Childre and Howard Martin,
> *The HeartMath Solution*

Whenever we face inner obstacles and become attached to landscapes like the Lower Self or the fear of death, there is always a remedy available. Just like the anti-life influence of the Lower Self, the fear of death is a resistance to living. One of the most powerful healing agents for the parts of us that resist life is gratitude. Gratitude is the positive force that transforms any part of us actively saying "no" to life. It evokes the sense that every moment of life is a treasure, with sensual riches to share. Gratitude is a quality of heart that reveals the significance of events and people in our life, as it adds meaning and appreciation to all that comes our way. It brings an experience of fullness to a mind perpetually hungry and discontent. It restructures our thinking, and breaks mental habits of discontent so that joy has more room to grow.

Gratitude is an antidote to fear. Feeling thankful quiets the negativity that spews from our minds in judgment, worry, and regret. Gratitude brings relief. It is the grease on the wheel of a lighted mind. When we acquire the habit of gratitude, uplifting, creative thinking replaces old ways of perceiving and therefore being. Riding this fluidity into action gives life more room to bring forth ease and positive outcomes. I have never seen someone with a physical disease cure themselves with negativity. Negative thinking supports the disease process, while a positive mentality, if authentic, leads to health. Focusing anxiously on the disease, dwelling on our fear of its outcome, obsessing about symptoms, and blaming ourselves for being sick, keep us stuck.

We all have negative thoughts. By adding gratitude to our daily rituals, we can catch these dark thoughts as they arise and, in that moment, choose to slip right back into a higher, fluid mind. When a feeling of gratitude infuses our thoughts, there is no need for the efforts of "staying positive" that so many of us have tried in the past. If positivity is forced, it becomes Pollyanna-ish and unreal. We must feel positive to truly think positively. As this affirmative energy grows in us, so does our "yes!" to life. This in turn changes the chemistry of the body. One moment of feeling positive is more healing than years of "brainstorming" about how to be healthy.

Healing My Fear of Death

The road to healing my own fear of death started with a health crisis. My body had become highly sensitive to most foods. I was limited for almost a full year to eating only vegetables and an occasional serving of meat. I was experiencing such strong states of deprivation, discouragement, and fear of death that I found myself locked in a state of depression that was hard to break. All I could think to do at this time was sit in meditation, go for long walks and stay open to my heart's guidance. I asked over and over for help in finding healing for this severe cycle I was in.

The turning point came one day, while hiking to Chimney Rock, one of my favorite trails. I had perched at the top of this overlook many evenings, watching the beautiful Sedona sunsets. As I arrived at my spot overlooking the valley that night, I heard a clear voice, like someone speaking right into my ear.

The voice said, "What is this deprivation giving you the opportunity to find in yourself?" A visual answer, an "aha" moment, came almost immediately. I saw myself receiving all that I needed to sustain life in a vibrantly abundant way. I finally understood what the struggle was all about. "Of course," I thought, "this isn't just some random event!" I realized how much I needed this experience of deprivation to come into more of a capacity for fulfillment. With this insight came enormous relief, and I felt my body relax and new energy pour in through the top of my head.

Sitting on that rock, I made the intention to work with my mind whenever I started to spin into negativity about my health. I reminded myself over and over again that this state was leading me into a deeply embodied experience of abundance and sustenance. Every time I felt deprived and fearful of malnourishment, I opened to feeling the abundance working its way into my body and mind. I fully felt myself moving into a higher state of being, and I felt thankful. Feeling gratitude for the entire experience helped me to hold this higher perspective— that the lower feeling states were coming forward for release as I stepped into a higher state of being. Within weeks of this insight, I was able to add more and more foods to my diet and literally receive the nourishment I had opened to.

Sometimes our bodies give us very clear signals about how we are resisting any form of life. It can be a very big wake-up call to realize that our negativity and fear of death are what keep us from health and life. Finding the higher road, the positive meaning, in even the harshest experiences can lead us toward enormous breakthroughs. The choice is ours to make.

When we pay attention to what the heart within each of us says about death, we can discover feelings of comfort and inspiration. We will hear statements that convey a broader view. The words might say, "Dear one, haven't you done this many times before? Have you not come and gone thousands of times in different guises?" The deepest place within us knows that we say hello and goodbye to our loved ones over and over again. We wear different costumes and play different roles, but we continue to step onstage and experience life in different forms. When this wheel of *samsara*, as Buddhists call it, comes to completion we move onto the next phase of evolution, as a more defined being, deeply knowing who we are in relation to life and existence and unity. We are our unique essence and with it fully intact, we merge deeper into the ecstasy of oneness.

Coming to Terms with Death

Death is the gate of life.
St. Bernard of Clairvaux

Coming to terms with death is an essential element to healing. As we come to accept death as a natural progression of physical life, we live life more fully. We cherish our time here with passion and hold it from the great perspective of continuity. Prying ourselves loose from the tight grip we have on survival, we begin to embody trust. This trust is a felt sense that all is as it should be. Trust gives us the knowing that we are an integral part of a broader spectrum of life, whether we are in a body or not. Learning to trust that we are held with the deepest, most tender care throughout our journey, whether we consistently feel this presence or not, allows for an unfolding within us. We can then unfasten our shackles and be alive and present in our life.

The restriction that we carry within our fear of death is a prison in our unconscious minds. As we let go, life-giving currents of energy flow through us and release us from attachment. New levels of freedom arise, and our inner warring, tensions, and identification with disease and disharmony melt away. And then, of course, the disease no longer has control over us. We relate to it differently. From this rarified place, healing, if it is of our highest will, takes place more easily.

As I've faced my own fear of death, I have found many patterns that my soul chose to experience. Early on, I became aware of an energetic residue around my heart and a numbing in my brain next to my temple. My mother has heart disease. She has had several near heart attacks and has had a stroke that affected this very place in her brain. Over the years, these genetically inherited places appeared in my body and mind. Emotional legacies from my mother, her mother, and my great grandmother came full circle through me.

At times, patterns stored in my DNA manifested in different areas of my body. Some nights I would wake up with what felt like arrhythmia; this is how my mother and grandmother's heart disease first appeared. My heart fluttered and skipped beats fairly often. Likewise, moments of aphasia, or difficulties processing and delivering communication, would arise in me the same way they have for my mother since her stroke. With inner work, I've systematically removed each little tendril that reached into my heart and organs or began to numb this area in my brain. Since facing my misperceptions about life and death, these troubled areas in my body and mind feel healthier, more vital, and clearer than before the symptoms first manifested. My physical symptoms have virtually dissolved.

While uncovering the layers of my fear of death brought significant healing to my body, it was when I released my fear of death for the first time that I came to a felt realization that I am borrowing this body. Finding acceptance for my imminent death was the moment I deeply chose life. In that moment I felt and intuitively saw an actual physical release of a genetic pattern in my DNA. The feeling that filled me was so freeing that I felt briefly what it must be like to release gravity altogether. My misperception of physical life as real and the soul as imagined fell away and suddenly I no longer had to hold on so tight.

We all have the ability to surrender our fear of death. When we die the little deaths of ego we gain strength of soul. It takes a warrior to walk through the emotions, the insults of daily life and come out the other side brighter and stronger as a result. At some point the shift comes. The ego, trying to convince itself of its permanence, is overshadowed by the indestructibility of the soul.

Chapter 7 Meditation
Exploring Our Fear of Death

We are all capable of letting go of our fear of death.
Until witnessed and released, it has control over us.

Crossing the thresholds of our immortality is not only
attainable to any who long for it, it is here now, within
us, in our deepest sense of freedom.

To begin:

First, intend that this meditation will bring clarity and
truth about unconscious fear that you have stored in
your system.

Find the warm depth of love and safety in your heart
and anchor into its presence.

When you feel relaxed and surrendered to The Love,
open your heart wide and let it hold you in its sacred
container.

Now become aware of any places in your body or mind holding fear.

With the light of your heart, venture into the tight, constricted place that is holding on for dear life. Feel the terror.

What is the most fearful thought you have about your own death? Harness your courage and strength and allow it forward into your awareness.

Now visualize this fearful scene and let yourself experience your death scenario fully while feeling the support and embrace of your Deep Heart.

Feel the fear and let the scenario unfold to its natural conclusion in your mind's eye.

Allow your heart to show you the continuation of your soul and its highest, most beautiful outcome.

Call forward deep gratitude for your life and all that it has brought you.

Now come into accepting life more deeply, being fully present in your life now, in this body.

Chapter 8

The Inner Chamber

Healing from the Inside Out

The Universe is Within

THE VEDAS

There is nothing more powerful than disease to re-mind us of how vulnerably human we are. During the process of medical treatment, if we choose this route, much of our time is spent sitting and waiting. We wait for the next doctor to see us, for lab results, or X-rays to be processed. We wait for prescriptions to be filled and for appointments to be rescheduled. These are times when we find ourselves feeling utterly dependent. De-pendent on an intern's assessment or a doctor's opinion. Dependent on family and friends for comfort. Dependent on insurance companies to cover our expenses.

Eventually we come to the understanding that no one

person or institution can fully meet our needs. Family might not be able to offer the kind of emotional support we long for. Doctors might not have all the answers. The money might not be there. The only dependable thing we can continually return to is the consistently giving, loving, and wise presence at our core. This is the one true reality, and it is only a breath away. We spend so much time waiting. Why not spend it receiving love, strength, and whatever else we need in every moment? When you relax into this inner resource, you, your life, and your situation can change dramatically.

Becoming the Love

> *Our life is shaped by our mind; we become what we think. Suffering follows an evil thought as the wheels of a cart follow the oxen that draw it.*

> *Our life is shaped by our mind; we become what we think. Joy follows a pure thought like a shadow that never leaves.*

> BUDDHA

What we feel inside, we become, and what we become, we draw to us as experience. Choose to become the love, the health that you long for. Choose it, and watch how the world responds differently to you, how outer and inner results begin to change. We have such a tremendous impact on our inner and outer environment, usually without even being aware of it. We can be compared to musical instruments; when one instrument in a room sends vibrations to other instruments in the same room, they "sing back" (or resonate at the same note) on their own, without being touched. Each part of the body responds to different tones or feelings in this same way. When we send a higher frequency feeling to a part of the body absorbed in a lower frequency thought or feeling, the lower resonance begins to vibrate with the higher, releasing its negative state. Love, joy, freedom, and peace are all examples of high-frequency states, while diseased areas and negativity are in a low-frequency state. Likewise, when we are resonating with positive feelings about health, we attract people with alternate views that open us to new ways to heal. We might be drawn to see a certain film that changes our perceptions or to a health practitioner who has a unique supplement. Or we might be inspired to try an herbal, homeopathic, or other approach that supports our health and relieves symptoms with no side effects.

We can personally access higher feeling states that magnetize the experiences we long for at any time. When we center within the high frequencies of the

Deep Heart, we not only find the power of harmonic manifestation, we can live in a state deeply rooted in love and power and wisdom. When our vision aligns with our center, we can see the higher truth or the bigger picture more easily. Likewise, we can see what is needed for healing in ourselves or in others. Our hearing, communication, awareness, and sense of smell and taste become heightened. We can actually hear a ring of truth or the disharmonic of dishonesty. We can smell fear or joy and clearly taste purity or impurity. We can feel subtle shifts of sensation, emotion, thought, and high qualities in ourselves and in others. We simply know how others feel and the quality of their thoughts because we know our own states so intimately. This brings us to states of unity, where we deeply understand ourselves to be a drop in the ocean, having a shared experience with everyone else.

Living from the center is literally living in a dimension where it becomes plainly obvious when something is of a higher frequency or when it is of an ego-centered reality. We gain the ability to discern between the Lower Self and Higher Self, the mask or authenticity, a mentalized state or a heartfelt one, moments of health and regeneration, and those of disease and decay. Our center is where we dissolve illusion and pierce into the clarity of bliss and health.

To have a practice of continually coming back to the core of our consciousness, to the Real Self within the heart center, is what changes life. This practice helps us to discover who we really are without the emotional charge, the mental machinations, and the physical pain. Imagine who you would be without the struggle. What would it feel like right now without disharmony, without disease in body, emotions, and mind? Let yourself have this feeling now. This is healing. The center point of you, around which all else revolves, is your beacon. It is your bliss, your peace and love, your power, your health. As we find the center point, anchor into it, and eventually become it, all else falls into place with complete ease.

The Heart's Witness

Wherever you go, go with all your heart.

CONFUCIUS

When we reach the capacity to witness our life, emotions, thoughts, and sensations from deep within the heart, we separate from the need to react to everything. We witness our human condition from deep inside our sacred chamber, immersed in peace. We start to feel liberated as we watch the old dramas unfold around us without feeling drawn into the circus and the struggle that ensue. The experience of witnessing from inside the heart is very different from evaluating from the mind. The mind can be aware of subtleties and patterns and sensations. It can be sharp in its analysis of internal reaction. However, observing the self from this vantage point, without having surrendered to the heart, leads to duality and separation. It lacks the breadth and the depth of the unified field of presence contained within the deep witness of the heart. When we experience witnessing from the heart, it reveals an unmistakable and extraordinary openness and clarity. The way becomes clear and joyful even when witnessing aspects of ourselves or others that are miserable! How healing it is to see our struggle and be able to laugh at it and share this common misery in our stories with others who are able to laugh about it too. Life is serious business and a hilarious chaotic ride. The more we can hold this paradox the more we are blessed with a state of well-being, that eventually turns into days and months of living in a harmonious flow. Even if you are unable to laugh and life feels serious and burdensome now, it's ok. Dive into the seriousness of it until it dissolves into a readiness to let go. Reaching this one of many peaks in awareness leads to a capacity to release the struggle against ourselves, while being amused by the drama of our old ways and adoring of our quirks and idiosyncrasies.

As you center into your true self and its heightened feelings of clarity and awe, it becomes very obvious what parts of you are not aligned with this state of harmony. The view from the center reveals all else that has yet to find its home. This is where our personal matrix comes into clear focus, and with practice we open to see, hear, know, or feel the disease pattern in all its manifestations. When we focus from this reference point we gain a growing awareness of how the disease resides in our mind or emotional body. A clear picture comes to us of how this connects to the diseased cells in our bodies. We locate the epicenter of our disease and see the misperceptions that hold its existence in place. Then our heart steps forward and disillusions us with the profound truth of benevolence and the unencumbered reality of a humble soul free from burdens. And this is all that is needed to wake up from the dream of this illness.

When we witness the whole picture of the disease from the presence of clarity within, we experience a vantage point from which all attachment to it, its emotional reality, moods, and beliefs have no strength over us. We will notice the habitual pull and the power this disease has had over us. We are used to taking its hand and letting it lead. No longer. Once the ultimate reality is glimpsed, our choice is plain and obvious. We can now see the man behind the curtain.

The Rhythms of Healing

Everything has rhythm. Everything dances.

MAYA ANGELOU

Sometimes we are able to disidentify from the disease relatively quickly. Other times it is a lifelong process. Either way, trust your deepest longing, and your individual pace will soon be established. Walking or running along this path at your own speed, you will find that there is a rhythm to the process. There is an inhale and an exhale. The times you break through and feel expanded, strong, and filled out with joy, will naturally be followed by a contraction. You might feel you are backsliding or that you have lost your way again. Remember, the pulsing rhythms of contraction and expansion are a part of the natural flow. The contraction gives us the opportunity to go inside again. This internal time is very sacred. When we find the insights and Healing Power waiting within the Deep Heart, the next expansion is on its way. The extent that we can bring love, awareness, and compassion to our pain in the down time is the extent to which we can embody the higher states when the next expansion comes. Eventually, both the inhale and the exhale are welcomed equally as an expression of love within the rhythm of life.

Relaxing into this flow will bring ease and grace. Sometimes it can be very difficult to trust the process when the inward movement comes. The child in us wants to feel good at all times! It helps to attune with the purpose of the soul through all the ups and downs and trust that this is leading us somewhere. Sufis refer to this cycle as walking through the fire of purification, and then resting and feeling the pleasure of the garden. Eventually we reach critical mass, or "the deep garden" of the heart. You will feel internally expanded in bliss, regardless of any emotional upheaval or mind state that appears on the surface. The deep knowing of your heart will become the friend that is always present. Even as your personality self occasionally responds out of habit, or you sink into a dark state for the time being, your inner knowing will be firm in the freedom from those old restraints. The better part of you resides in your center, while the rest of you dwells in a state of refinement and integration. An enormous sense of relief is waiting for you with this deep knowing that the sacred fire cooks your ego as a feast for your soul!

Chapter 8 Meditation
The Inner "I"

This meditation requires calling all awareness to center. Once we set our compass toward the deepest heart center, and walk, and keep walking, we will find ourselves deep inside our core of light where all outside of it becomes clear. Set a strong intention for this depth, and trust that you will arrive here. Your heart is the beacon.

Drop in to the deep heart. With each breath, go deeper and deeper into the clean, open reality of the deep heart.

Find the feeling sense of it and sink in.

Become it.

Bring all points of awareness into this centered still point in your heart, so that it is your only reference point.

Beneath the mind.

Beneath the emotions.

Open the eye of your heart now, and look from this central vantage point at the periphery of your being.

Pull back even further into your true strength and take in the reality of this disease or condition from the inside out. This central point is your deepest, clearest consciousness.

Scanning your body from the inside, locate the grid or network that consists of the emotional, mental, and physical aspects of this disease or condition.

Now that you have pulled back far enough to look it in the eye and see it as something other than you, take a long look. See it in its entirety. If this disease were a person or other sentient being, what does it look like?

What does it want?

How does having this condition serve you?

Feel the pull it has on you to identify with it.

Disconnect from it and come back to the core of you.

Allow the insights forward about your condition.

Feel the essence of this depth pouring forward and feeding your body and mind in every moment in every way, giving you all that you need to heal now.

Become this essence. Know that this is the truth of who you are.

Bathe the periphery of you, the mind, the emotional self in this essential light.

Expand it into your energy field, two feet out from your body, three feet, four feet, five feet.

Vibrate in the reality of The Love.

Take deep breaths now.

Feel your physical presence absorbed in light.

Skin, muscles, organs, bones.

Feel the weight of your physical matter on the cushion beneath you.

Become aware of your material surroundings.

Bring yourself back into the room, your life, your day.

Open your eyes when ready and bring your existential truth with you into this life in your world.

Chapter 9

Surrendering to Love's Will

The Spiritual Purpose of Disease

> *When you have come to the edge of all the light*
> *you have*
> *And step into the darkness of the unknown*
> *Believe that one of the two will happen to you*
> *Either you'll find something solid to stand on*
> *Or you'll be taught how to fly!*
>
> RICHARD BACH

Uncovering our innate essence lies at the heart of this path to health. We are called to find our personal experience of transcendent healing on all levels, to clean house in mind, body, emotion, and soul. The potent energy source in our hearts has a customized gift of healing for each one of us. Whatever we might need, the

Deep Heart has more than enough. It holds the kind of power that can reach through our biggest blocks, transform our thinking and emotions, and heal us physically if it is of its higher will. It acts of its own high perception, one that holds a reality beyond all limitation. This is the truest version of you.

Many of us pray, "God, please take this disease from me." When the condition remains, we see God as cruel or ourselves as failures. This response stems from a misperception of our Higher Power as separate from us, and disease (in any form) as an enemy, its purpose to punish or torture us. Disease is a companion on a deep and sacred path, compelling us toward greater realization of our true nature and its source. Through this path we find our meaning and our grace.

The stark truth of our mortality comes forward, hand in hand with the essence of ongoing life. This discovery transcends any anger or judgment we have toward one another or ourselves, the separation we have carried in our minds. We begin to see that we are not our bodies alone and realize that the purpose of life is not to maintain superficial happiness. The gifts, if we open to them, are endless. The deeper movement of the heart will take us to the most sublime of places, if we only allow it to do so.

Choosing to surrender to this experience gives us our greatest chance at maintaining and manifesting health and conditions for health on all levels. And then we discover that physical health is not our main goal after all. Living in the reality of Oneness, either within form or without form, is what we most deeply long for. Our physicality is merely a means to this end without end.

The infinite in us might say, "If living the path of dis-ease and eventually leaving my body behind gives me the knowing of a soulful existence, then so be it." This is not to be glib about such a deeply challenging process, but to find the perspective of the higher consciousness within us. Our higher self would sacrifice anything: wealth, health, relationships, even physical life, to attain true love, intimacy, and authentic presence of mind through its physical form.

Moving On

We are not human beings having a spiritual experience. We are spiritual beings having a human experience.

TEILHARD DE CHARDIN

Alena

I first met my dear friend Alena while we both were students attending an energy healing school. She was a spiritually developed soul, and we connected deeply, sharing many meaningful experiences together over time. More than once over the years, Alena remarked to me that she felt unable to really deeply connect to subtle energies. She so wanted to be able to feel the hearts of people around her and to perceive energetic subtleties within others, wherever they were. Yet this deep intimacy with life felt out of her reach, and she knew that her overactive mind stood in her way. I remember Alena once complaining that she just felt blocked in her head, that her mind was so stubborn she couldn't see her way around or through it.

Not long after that conversation, Alena was diagnosed with a tumor on her brain stem. Naturally, cancer was a devastating reality for her to swallow at first, and it took all of her strength to wake up every morning to face it. With time, however, she began to experience deeper and deeper levels of letting go, leading to greater and greater transformation.

Alena visited many alternative healers who had dissolved tumors and offered cures not yet available to Western medicine. As she searched for answers, she spent valuable time with family and friends who traveled from across the country to be with her. Along with chemotherapy, Alena embraced every mode of healing that she knew to come back to health and remove the tumor. As she faced negative thinking, many deep-rooted emotional patterns were healed. She unearthed places within her soul that were lost in illusion and integrated them through The Love. As she flushed out old, stuck ways of being one by one, she started to feel lighter than ever before. Life began to shine with new color. With each understanding that came her way, she perceived her mortality in a new light.

In her final month of life in its physical form, Alena experienced a deep and profound shift. Life opened in an unexpected and miraculous way. She had spent so much time receiving love and healing, the stuck feeling that she had worked with for so long unraveled into an unrecognizable form. She found herself receiving love deeply and profoundly, as she released all the ways she had kept it at bay through the years. Speaking with Alena was a different experience entirely; she was able to open her heart so fully that the warmth and love emanating from her filled the room like sun pouring through a window. Her time with others became rich and alive and deeply fulfilling.

The last time we spoke, Alena mentioned that she had never in her life felt so open and aware. Her mind no longer stood in the way. She was finally able to feel the presence of everyone in her life, wherever they were, as though they were standing right next to her. In line at the grocery store, she'd feel an energy healer friend working on her back. In another moment, she could sense her mother's concern. In the next, her teacher's voice would come to her, clearly stating an offering of wisdom she could use in that moment.

She was not only aware of herself and her loved ones in new ways, she also understood that her new home, in a different realm, awaited her. She began to recognize through her heart that her death was approaching. She also became aware that her death would merely be a transition to an entirely new life. She would only be shedding a skin. Along with her newfound ability to feel connected to life, she became open to connecting with the reality beyond death. All the healing Alena received was a blessing; it brought her deep transformation, and fulfilled her longing for Oneness. And finally, what became clear was that the soul we called Alena was ready to move on.

The gift Alena gave so many of us with her passing was the deep acceptance of and respect for her soul's *purpose. It was awe-inspiring to witness. The feeling of elation and celebration when she transitioned from this realm to the next was palpable for all who were able to perceive it. My every cell tingled with visions of light and the complete freedom in which she was immersed. Others mentioned that afterward she came to them in dreams, sharing the wisdom she found in her transition to the unseen worlds.*

For some, the purpose of disease is to awaken lost parts of the self that are ready to be brought into their life, in order to heal and continue on in a body. For others, like Alena, as the awakening occurs, it becomes clear that a new journey awaits after death. As we open to trust that our true nature is leading us, we grow to accept that either way, all is as it should be. This body suit that we zip into and out of might need some repair, or it might be time for us to leave it behind. Either way, its true purpose is to serve the soul within it.

Chapter 9 Meditation
Your Soul's Purpose

Trust and listen. All that The Beloved of your heart knows you are ready to receive, it will reveal.

Relax your mind and enter your heart.

Connect to your inner healing power.

Feel the deep ocean of omnipresence and love in your heart.

Drop deeper now into this source, this liquid healing light.

Ask it, "What is it that I am longing for the most in my life? What is my deepest purpose?"

Open to the quality of feeling that comes with the answer. The answer might simply be the quality of feeling for now.

Is it clarity? Purity? Vitality? Power? Inspiration? Surrender? Love?

Sit now in gentle receptivity and await the response of your heart.

Whatever the answer, bring the quality of feeling to the areas of your body or mind that need this medicine.

Place your hands on these areas and allow the healing current to flow from your heart, through your arms and out your hands and into the places that need it the most.

Allow and receive it.

If your mind is busy and congested, place your hands on your head and relax your brain tissue into this silent surrender, bowing your head to your heart.

Allow the soothing light to penetrate the areas of your body and mind that have not seen healing light and have needed it for so long.

If emotions or thoughts are arising, allow room for them to express, feel them fully, and then release them to the strong yet gentle hands of the healer. Letting down … letting go …

That's right, you are creating more room for The Love to fill you, taking up residence in your body and bringing you pure love, joy, and fulfillment.

Invite this higher healing presence to come forward to express through your body and mind.

Intend to bring this deep internal presence into a tangible physical experience in your life.

Know that you are held always, completely, and in every way.

About the Author

My own journey of the deep heart inspired the writing of this book. My longing and love guided me through the heartbreak and exhilaration. It led me to the discovery of profound peace and love that comes with being very human, and it has now led my words to you. May this book serve to help you find the healing, love and peace you seek.

Anne has a private practice on Maui doing conscious healing session work. In 2007, she founded The School of the Deep Heart, offering healing retreats and work-shops locally and overseas. Anne holds a masters in

Contemplative Psychotherapy, a degree in Body/Mind Psychotherapy, a degree in Transpersonal Hypnosis and a four year degree in Conscious Healing. Conscious Healing is the basis for deep heart work and her healing approach. For audio meditations and teachings, to sign up for Anne's newsletter and for more information go to: www.schoolofthedeepheart.com.

LaVergne, TN USA
13 October 2009
160707LV00001B/1/P